HELP! THERE'S A DRAGON IN MY HEAD

WRITTEN BY
JAN ESH &
STEPHEN NAUTA

ILLUSTRATIONS BY
CHRISTI DREESE

Help, There's A Dragon in My Head

Copyright © by Stephen Nauta and Jan Esh
ISBN: 978-1-939294-25-8

All rights reserved. No part of this book may be reproduced or transmitted in any form or by any means without written permission of the authors.

Illustrations by Christi Dreese

Cover design by Christi Dreese
Graphic Design by Jacob Kubon

Published by

Splattered Ink Press

Splatteredinpress.com

Dedication

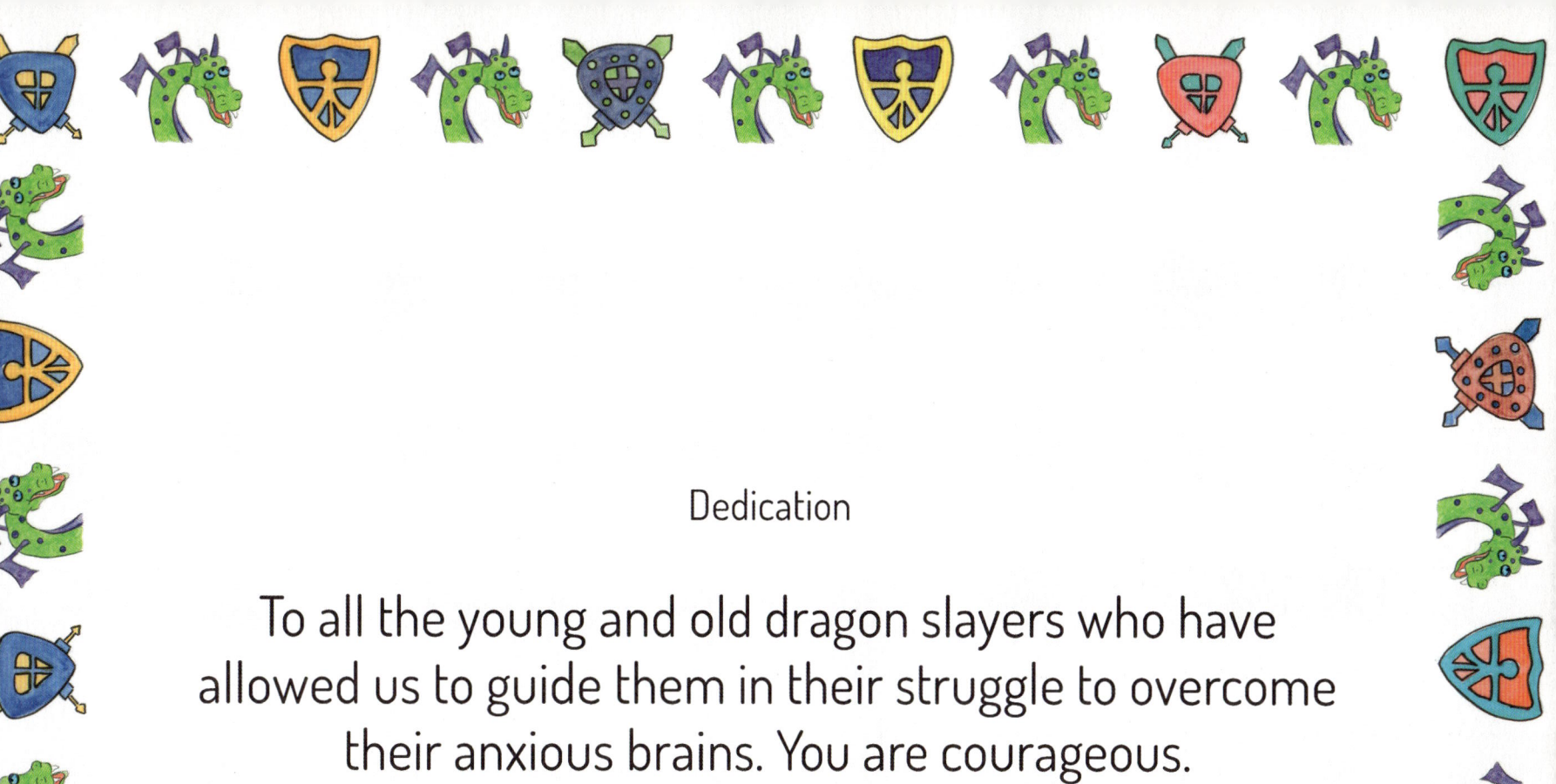

To all the young and old dragon slayers who have allowed us to guide them in their struggle to overcome their anxious brains. You are courageous.

There is a dragon in my head and he is mean.

He says he is my best friend.

He says he wants to take care of me and keep me safe.

But I don't believe him.

Don't tell him though, because I hate it when he gets angry at me.

My dragon is bossy and always tells me –

What to do or not do.

What to say or not say.

What to play or not play.

Who to talk to, who to ignore.

What to wear or not wear.

When to laugh and when to frown.

When to feel safe and when to feel afraid.

When to be happy and when to be sad.

When to walk and when to run.

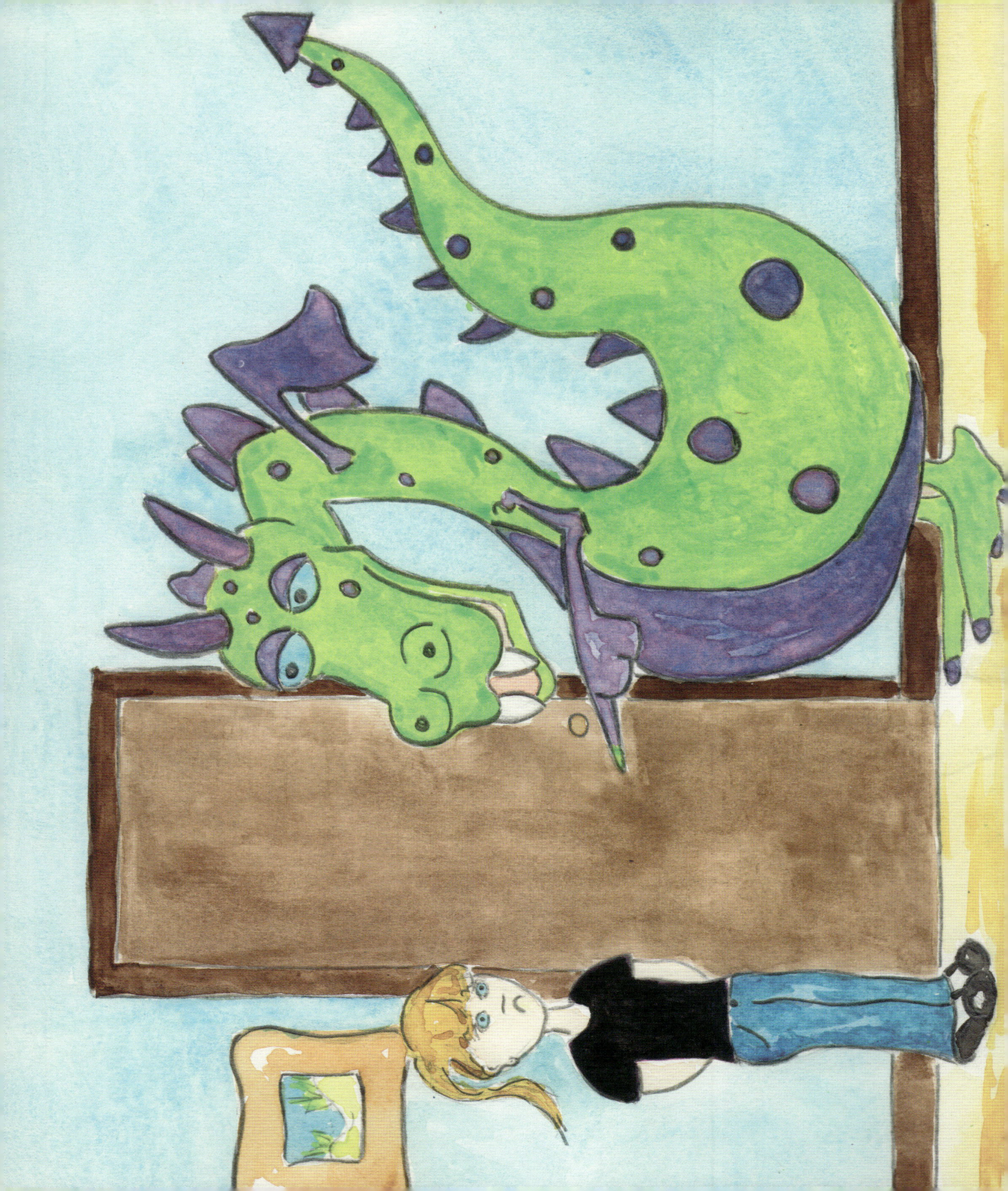

My parents don't even boss me around like that.

My dragon doesn't like my parents.

He doesn't like my friends' parents, my aunts, uncles, teachers, babysitter, soccer coach, or piano teacher.

"Don't trust anyone," he says. "I am the only one who cares about you. I know what is best for you."

I think he wants to be the boss of my life.

When I get ready for school, I pick out my favorite outfit.

It is a short purple skirt with pleats and a fancy top with tons of sparkles.

I ask my mom if my hair looks okay.

"I love it when you wear your hair in pigtails," she says.

She takes both of my pigtails in her hands and tickles my face with them.

"Better watch out for those boys today," she says.

"She didn't tell you that the boys are going to play tug-of-war with your head," my dragon says.

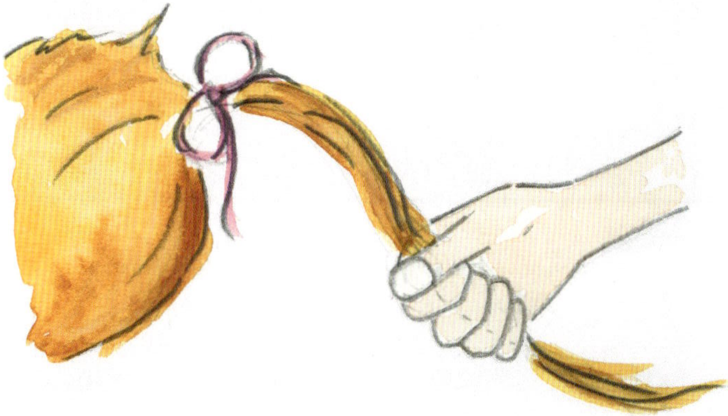

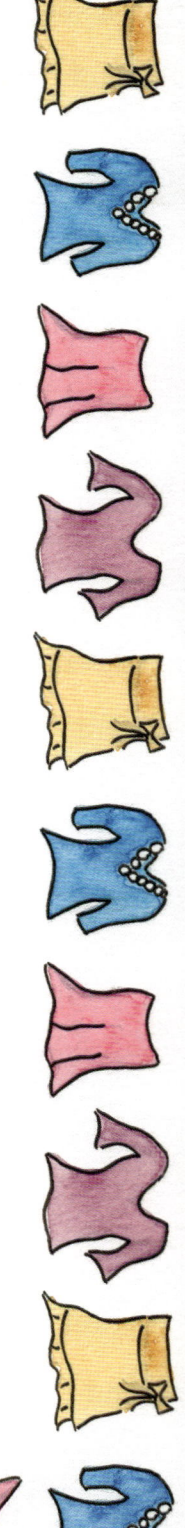

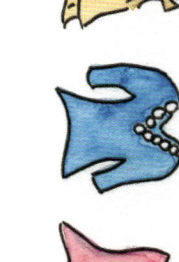

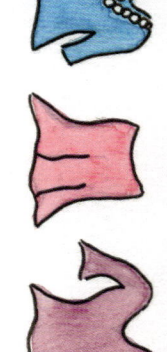

silly, silly, silly... silly, silly, silly... silly, silly, silly...

I ask my dad if my outfit looks pretty.

"Let me see. Walk toward me and twirl like a model," he says.

I put my hands on my cheeks and plaster a big smile on my face.

I swing my hips from side to side and start to twirl.

"Stop that. You look silly," my dragon says. "Besides you might just trip and fall when you twirl."

I stop.

"I hate it when you make me do silly things like this," I yell at my dad. "Why can't you just answer my question?"

silly, silly, silly... silly, silly, silly...

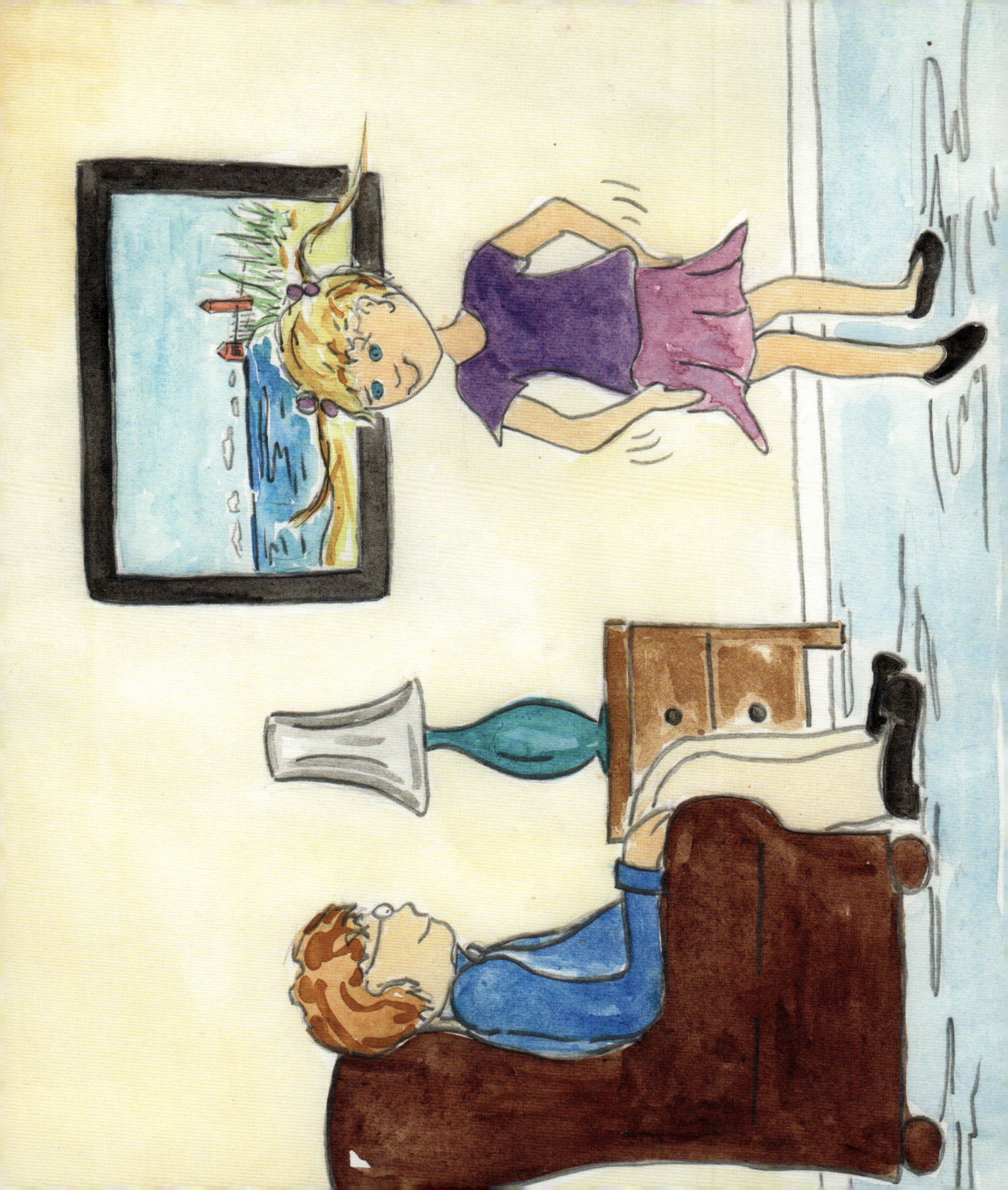

"Sorry," he says. His eyes open wide and they look a little wet.

"I just think you look gorgeous in that outfit and you should be a little flashy," my dad says. "Show it off to the world so they can see what I see."

I feel sorry for yelling at my dad.

"Don't fall for that act," my dragon says. "He's just saying that because he doesn't want to hurt your feelings. You look absolutely ridiculous in that get-up."

I avoid my dad's sad eyes by looking at the ground as I go to my room.

I change into my boring jeans and black t-shirt.

I put my hair into my regular old ponytail.

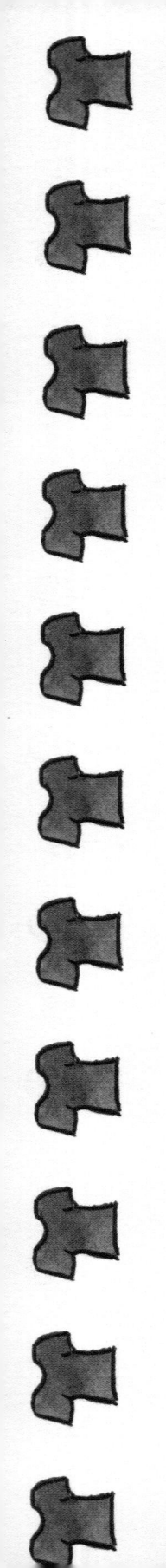

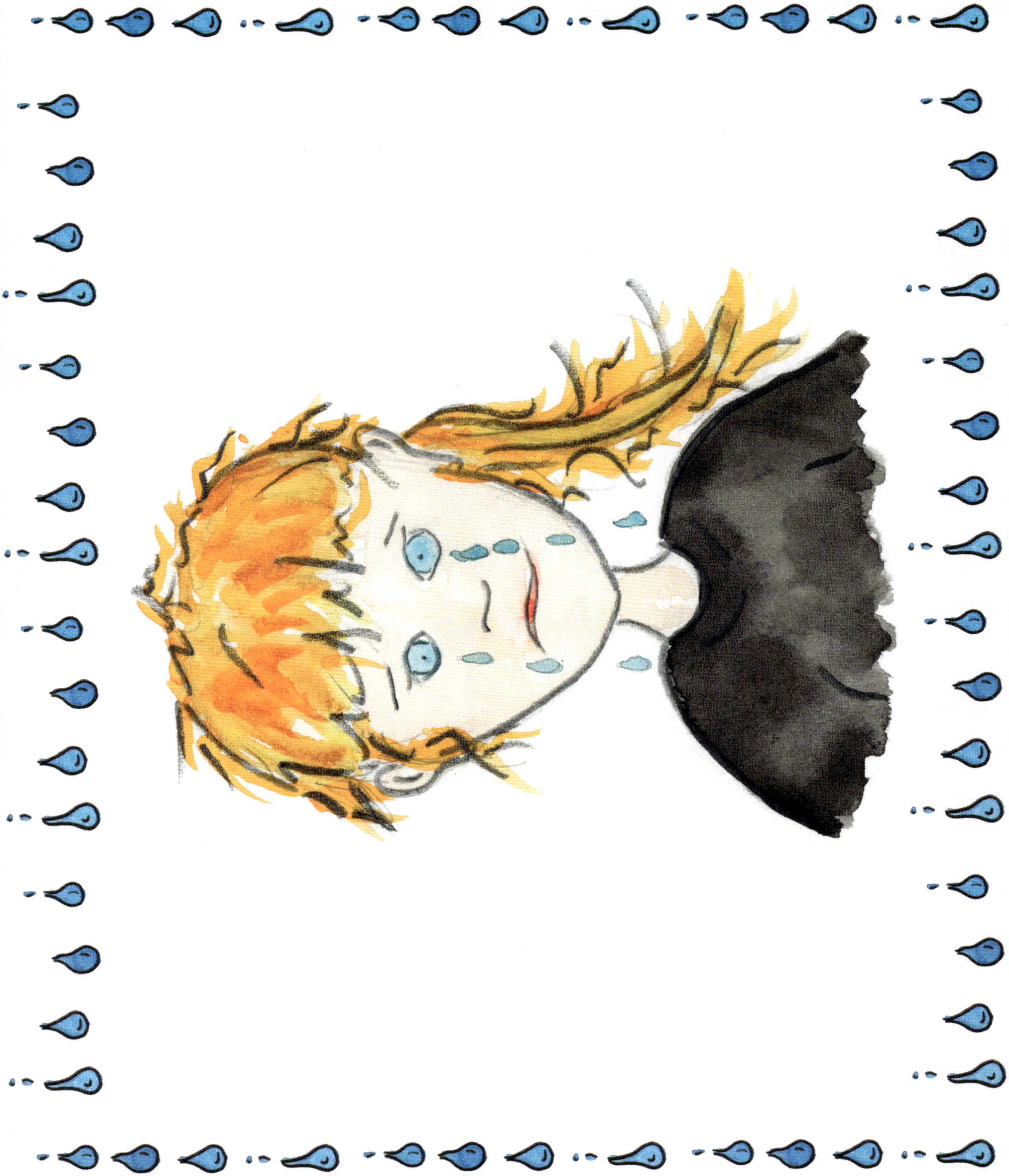

I get a B on my science project, and I always get A's on everything.

"I can't believe how dumb you are," my dragon says. I start to cry.

Ms. Blakely comes over to me.

"It's okay to get a B," she says. "You don't have to be perfect."

"Don't listen to her!" my dragon screams at me. "She doesn't know you like I do. If you aren't perfect, everyone will see what I see. They will see that you act like a smarty-pants, but underneath it all you are a stupid little girl!"

My dragon is furious.

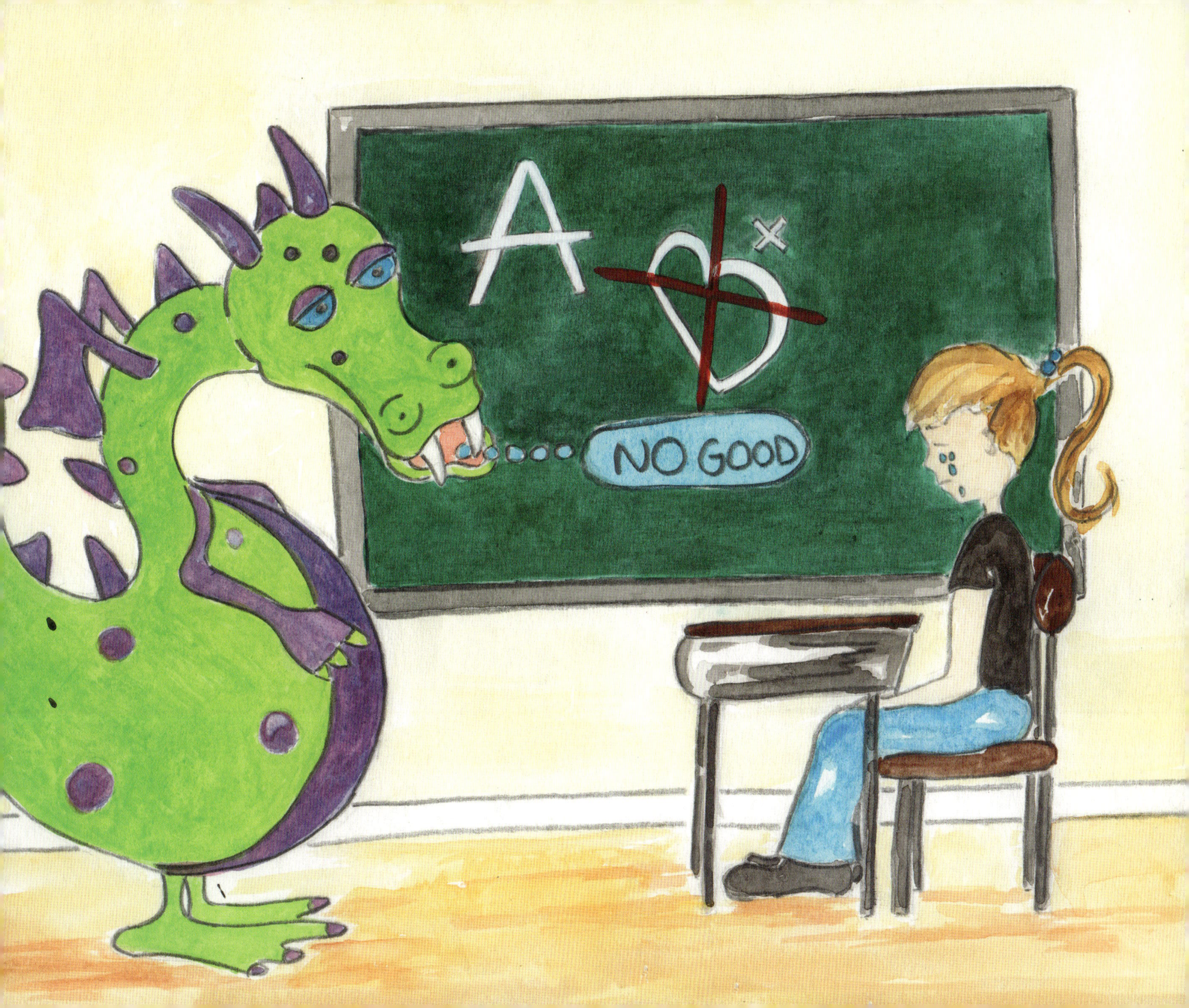
A
NO GOOD

No Friends... No Friends... No Friends... No Friends... No Friends... No Friends... No Friends... No Friends... No Friends... No Friends... No Friends... No Friends... No Friends... No Friends...

My dragon doesn't want me to have friends.

He tells me shy is good because shy is safe.

But being all by myself at recess isn't fun.

You have No Friends...

Local comedian gets a standing ovation at the State Theatre. Local comedian does stand up to an over following audience at local restaurant. Local comedian gives impression of grandmother to a standing room only crowd!

I can be funny sometimes; like when I make my parents laugh.

I do my impression of Grandma complaining about her neighbors and my parents roll on the floor laughing.

"You should be a comedian," my mom says.

I think I can make my friends laugh, too.

"Parents are an easy audience," my dragon says. "Your friends will laugh at you, not with you."

My dragon shakes his head.

"Remember first grade? When you tried to tell your dad's monkey joke? Nobody laughed."

I slump my shoulders and resign myself to always being alone.

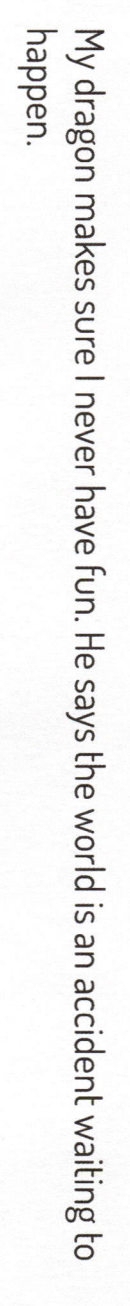

My dragon makes sure I never have fun. He says the world is an accident waiting to happen.

Once my cousins were bouncing up and down on the trampoline my parents bought me. They were laughing the whole time. One even tried a flip. He didn't make it and I was glad nothing broke on his body.

I sat on the porch with my dragon and just watched.

I kept feeling like something bad was going to happen.

"Come jump with us," they called out to me.

My dragon reminded me of the impending disaster.

"I don't want to jump right now," I said.

It was a big fat lie. I wanted to join them on my trampoline, but it was too risky.

So I safely watched from the sideline with my dragon.

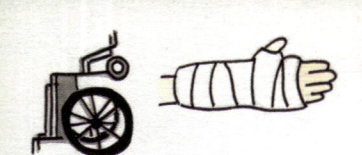

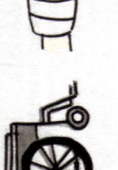

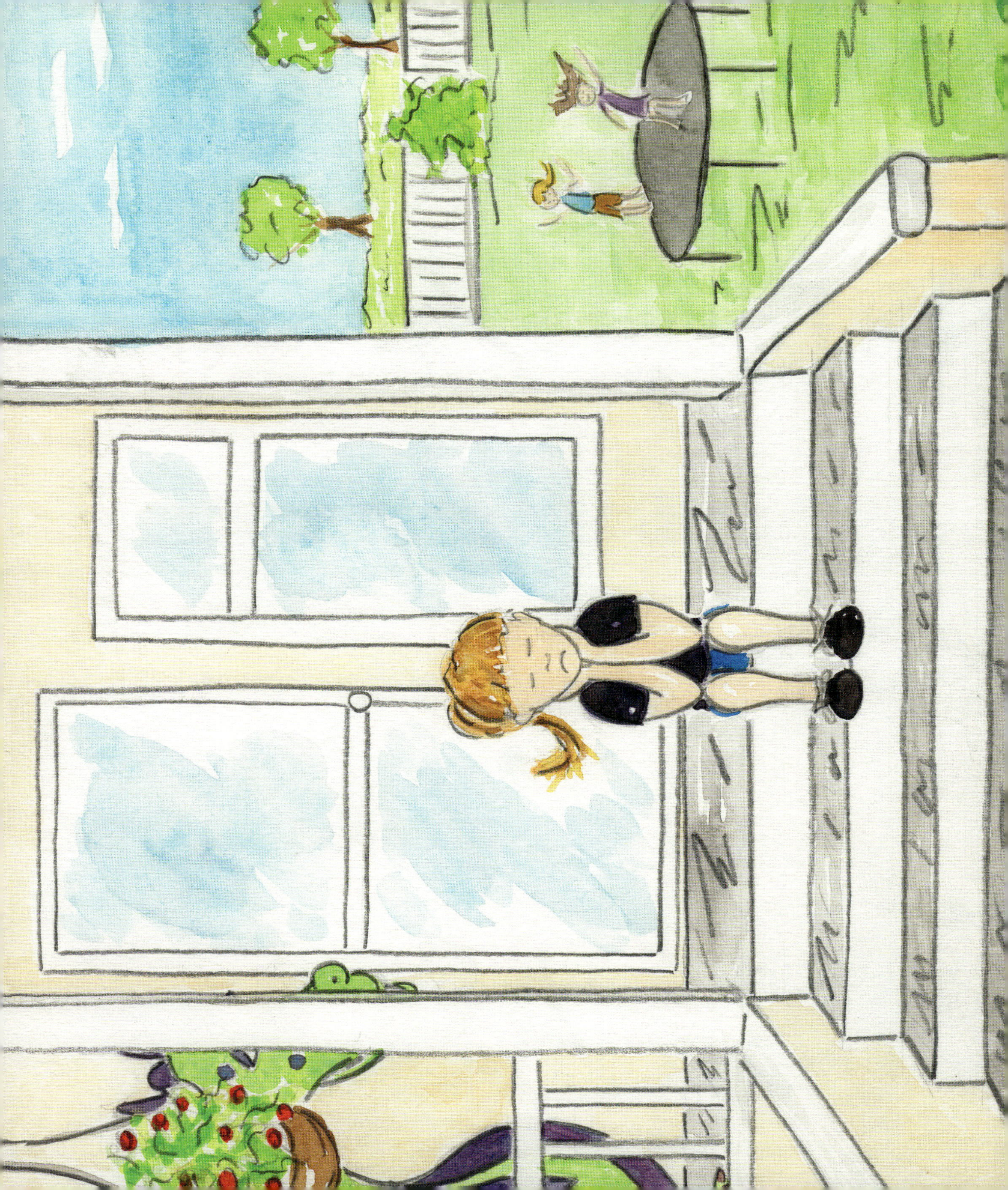

so embarrassing . . . so embarrassing . . . so embarrassing . . . so embarrassing . . . so embarrassing . . .

Another time I tried to spend the night at my friend Lucy's house.

Embarrassing is all I can say about that adventure.

Ten minutes into the night my dragon whispered into my ear, "I wonder what your mom is doing. Do you think she is okay?"

I started to freak out.

"She could be dead for all you know," he said.

I got so worried I thought I might pee my pants.

"What if you wet the bed?" my dragon asked.

I never wet the bed, I thought.

"What if tonight is different?" my dragon said.

What if I get so nervous I wet the bed? And what if the kids at school find out? What if they point at me and laugh at recess?

I woke up my friend and she took me to her mom, who called my mom, who picked me up in her pajamas (they are kind of raggedy), and took me home—which is where I spend all of my nights in the company of my dragon, who I can't stand.

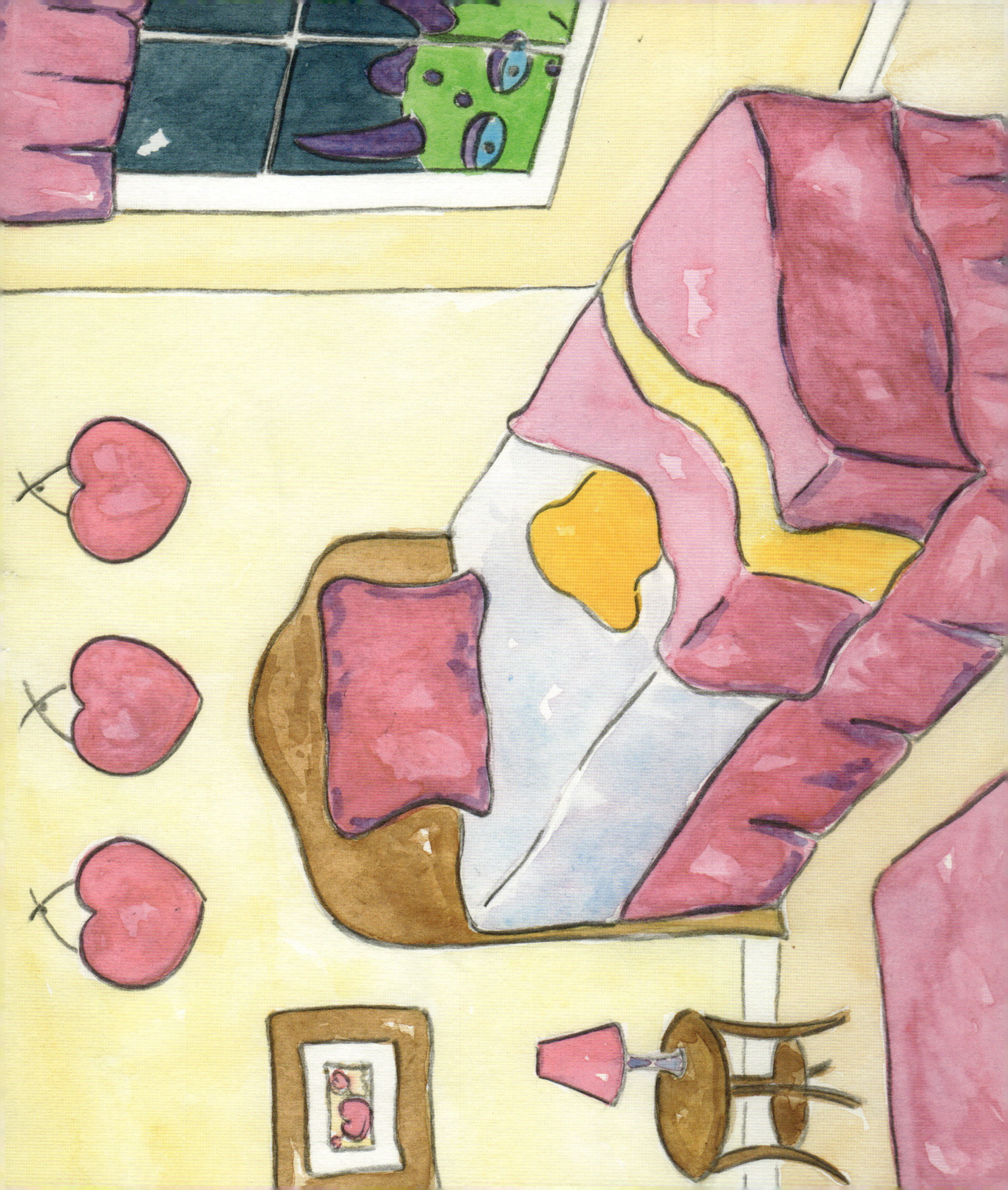

12345... 12345... 12345...

My dragon makes me do weird things over and over again. He does this by making bargains with me.

"If you count to five out loud every time you feel worried, you will be safe," he says.

I try and it works. I feel safe.

But everyone stares at me, which makes me very uncomfortable.

I try to whisper in a soft voice so all I do is move my lips, but no matter how I turn my face, someone always notices.

"Why do you move your lips that way?" they ask.

"I don't know what you are talking about," I say as I walk away mumbling.

"You're doing it again," they shout back.

I wish I could be invisible.

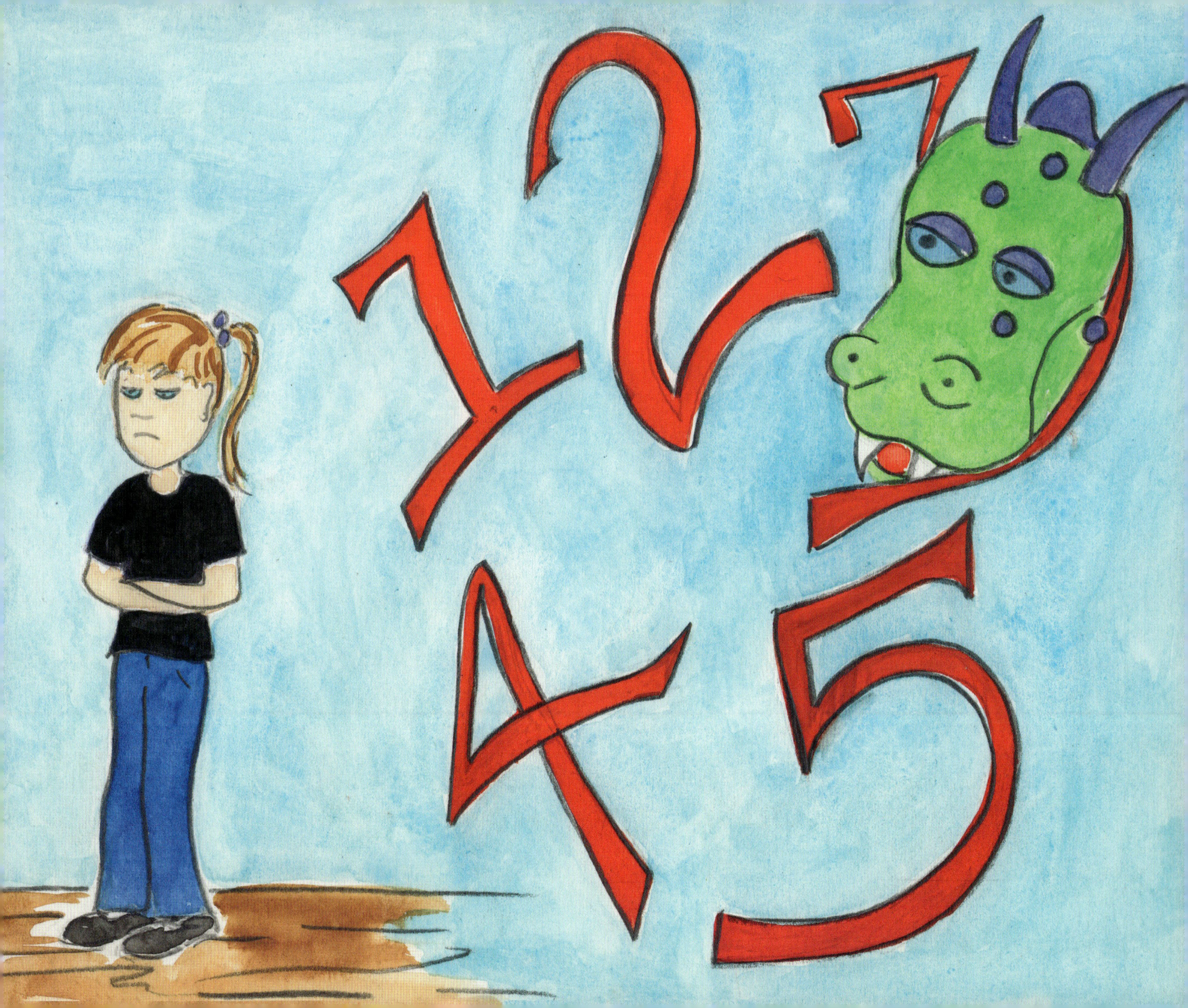

1 2 7
4 5

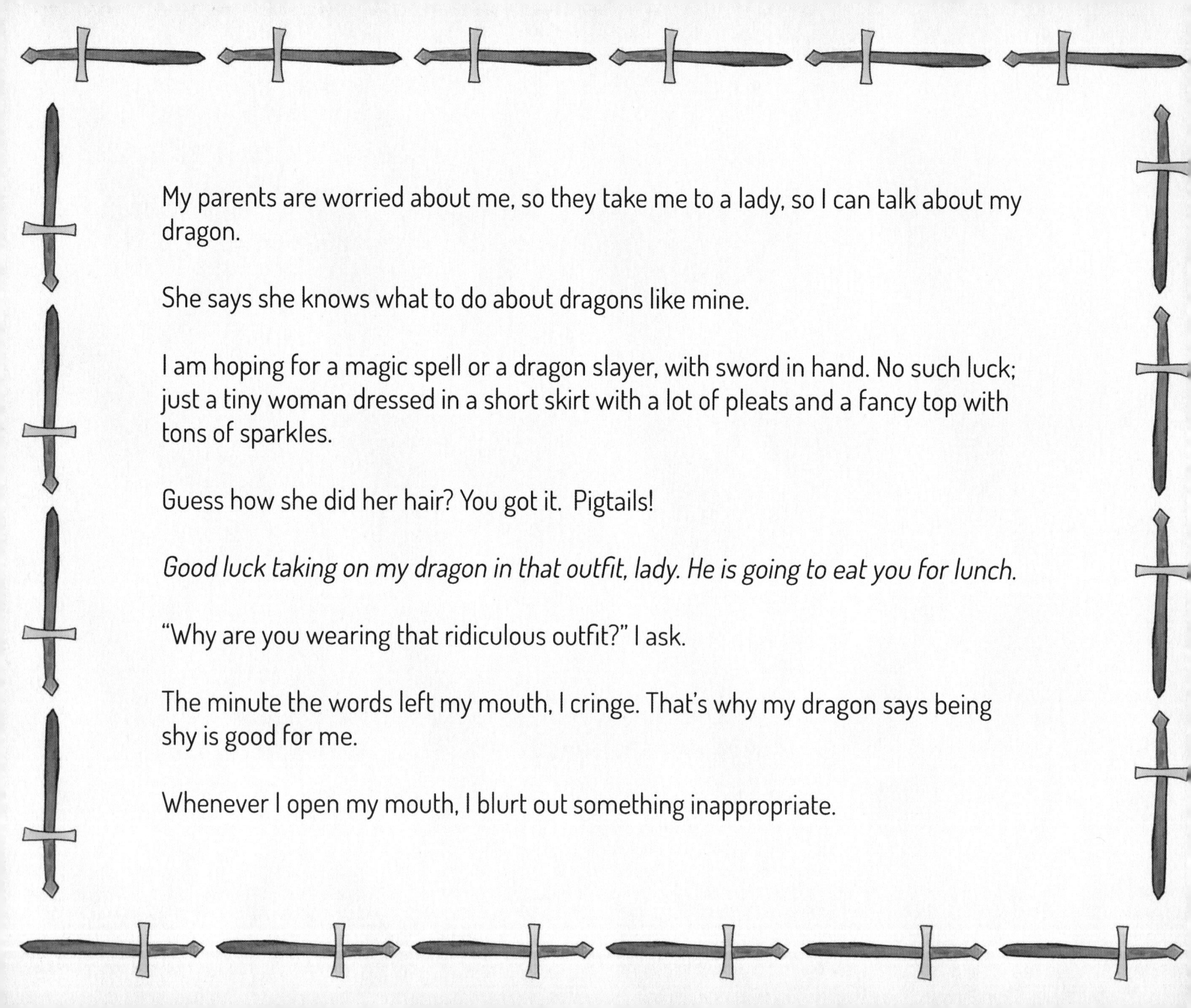

My parents are worried about me, so they take me to a lady, so I can talk about my dragon.

She says she knows what to do about dragons like mine.

I am hoping for a magic spell or a dragon slayer, with sword in hand. No such luck; just a tiny woman dressed in a short skirt with a lot of pleats and a fancy top with tons of sparkles.

Guess how she did her hair? You got it. Pigtails!

Good luck taking on my dragon in that outfit, lady. He is going to eat you for lunch.

"Why are you wearing that ridiculous outfit?" I ask.

The minute the words left my mouth, I cringe. That's why my dragon says being shy is good for me.

Whenever I open my mouth, I blurt out something inappropriate.

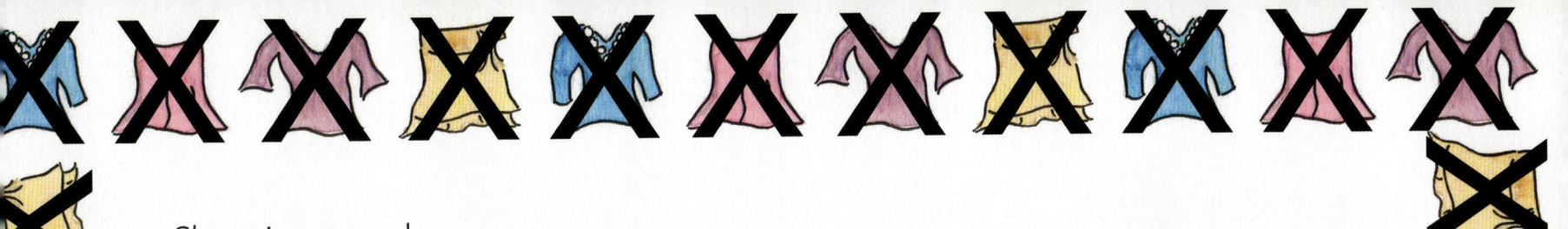

She spins around.

"You don't like my outfit?" She has a soft voice that makes me feel calm.

"It's not that. It's just that...don't people think you look ridiculous?"

She looks me in the eye and for some reason I don't feel like I have to look away.

"If they do, they don't say so. And even if they did, why would I care?" she says. "I like dressing like this. It makes me feel good; like I'm celebrating life."

This woman gets me.

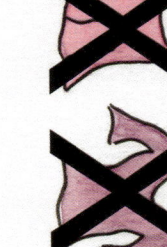

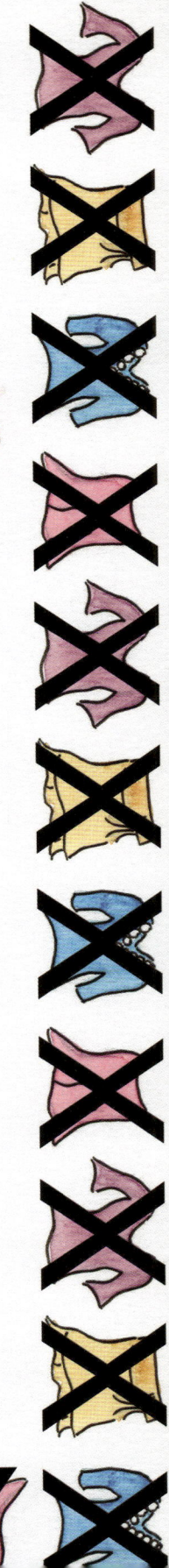

"You should try dressing in a way that makes you feel good."

She motions for me to sit.

"I couldn't do that."

I look at my knees, which are covered by my boring jeans.

"Why not?" she asks.

"Lie, lie, lie," my dragon says.

I take a chance on this soft-spoken, extravagantly-dressed, self-proclaimed dragon slayer, because I like her soothing voice.

"I've got a dragon in my head and he won't let me," I say. "He says I would look ridiculous and everyone would laugh at me."

She is not fazed by what I tell her. In fact, she acts like she knows him.

"What else has he told you?" she asks.

I try to speak, but I can't. The words won't come out. I can't betray my dragon.

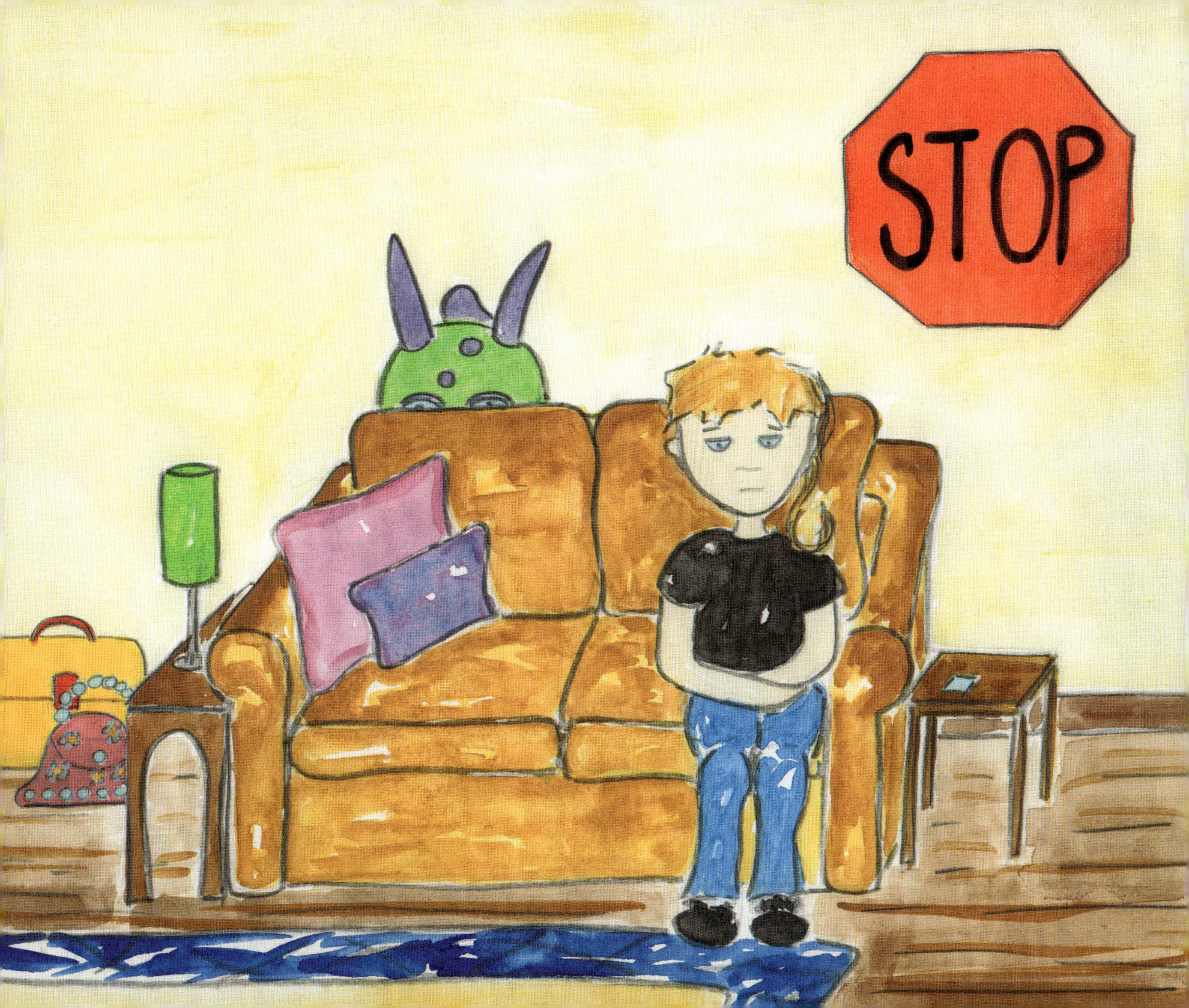
STOP

crazy... crazy... crazy... crazy...

She starts to tell me almost word-for-word everything my dragon has ever said to me.

It is like she has a dragon of her own. For the first time in my life I consider the possibility that I might not be crazy.

"Do you know my dragon?" I ask.

"I do," she says, "and it is time we get him out of your head. He doesn't belong there."

"How can I do that?"

"Just ask him."

"But he won't leave, I've tried," I say.

"He will if you insist."

"I don't know."

"How about we start by giving him a name? A mean name that reflects who he is."

"How about Bob?"

"It has to be nasty, mean."

"How about Dumbo?"

"Why Dumbo?"

"That's what my friends and I used to call a boy in our class who was a big bully."

"Dumbo it is," she says.

I grin from ear to ear, and then it hits me.

I haven't thought about my dragon, I mean Dumbo, since I started listening to my new friend.

Maybe she is a dragon slayer.

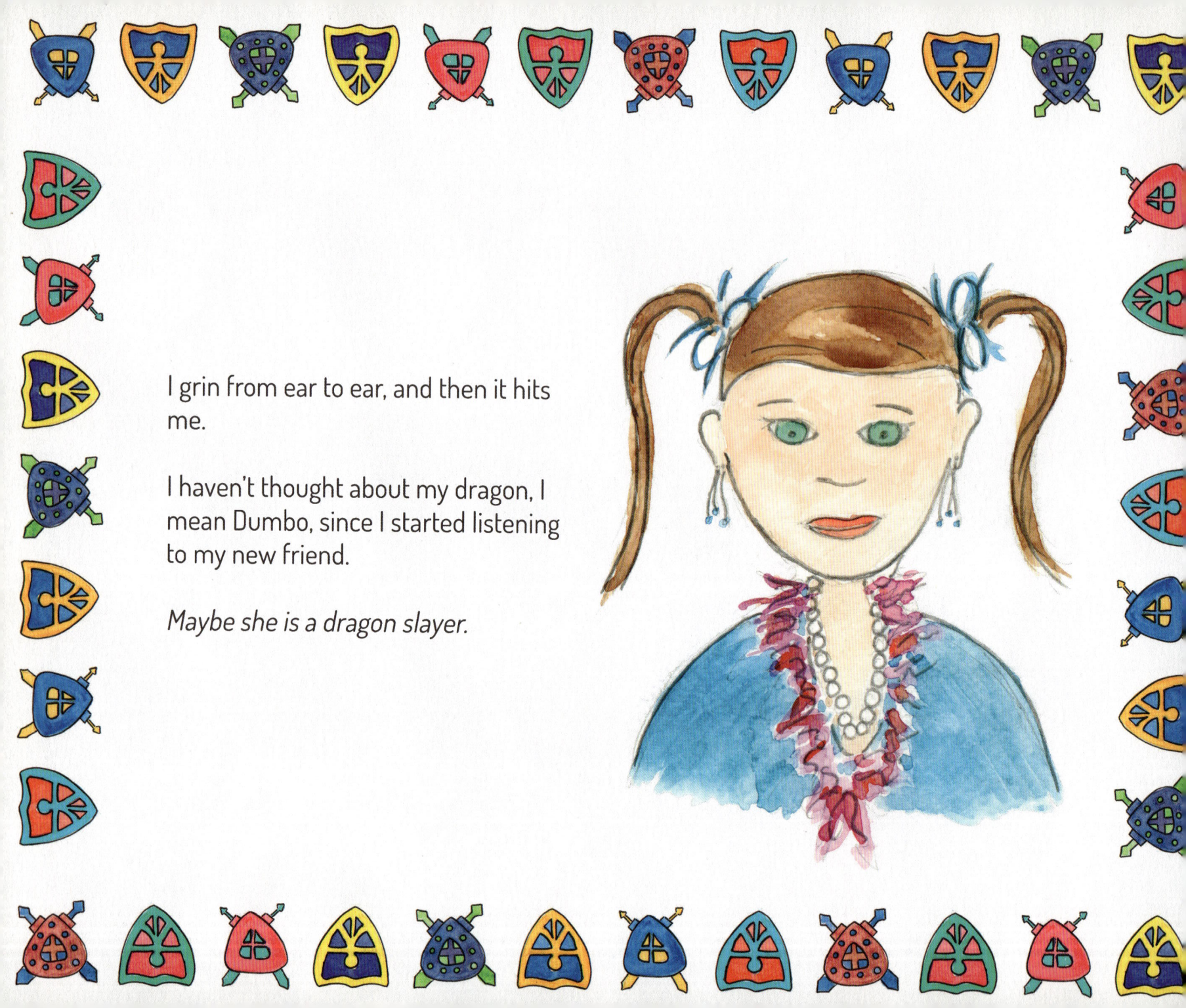

You're different... You're stupid... You're gullible...

I skip out of her office and into my mother's arms. I can't remember the last time I felt this free.

However, the minute I get into the car, my brain hits reverse.

Dumbo, I mean my dragon, is back in full force.

"So you think your new friend can get rid of me just by calling me a mean name. You are so gullible," he says. "You know what that means? It means you're stupid enough to think a silly little woman knows more than me."

He crosses his arms and gives me a mean look.

"Those tricks might work for other kids, but you are different. They won't work for you," he says. "You think she cares about you? Well, she doesn't. At least not like I care about you."

So much for the sweet-talking dragon slayer.

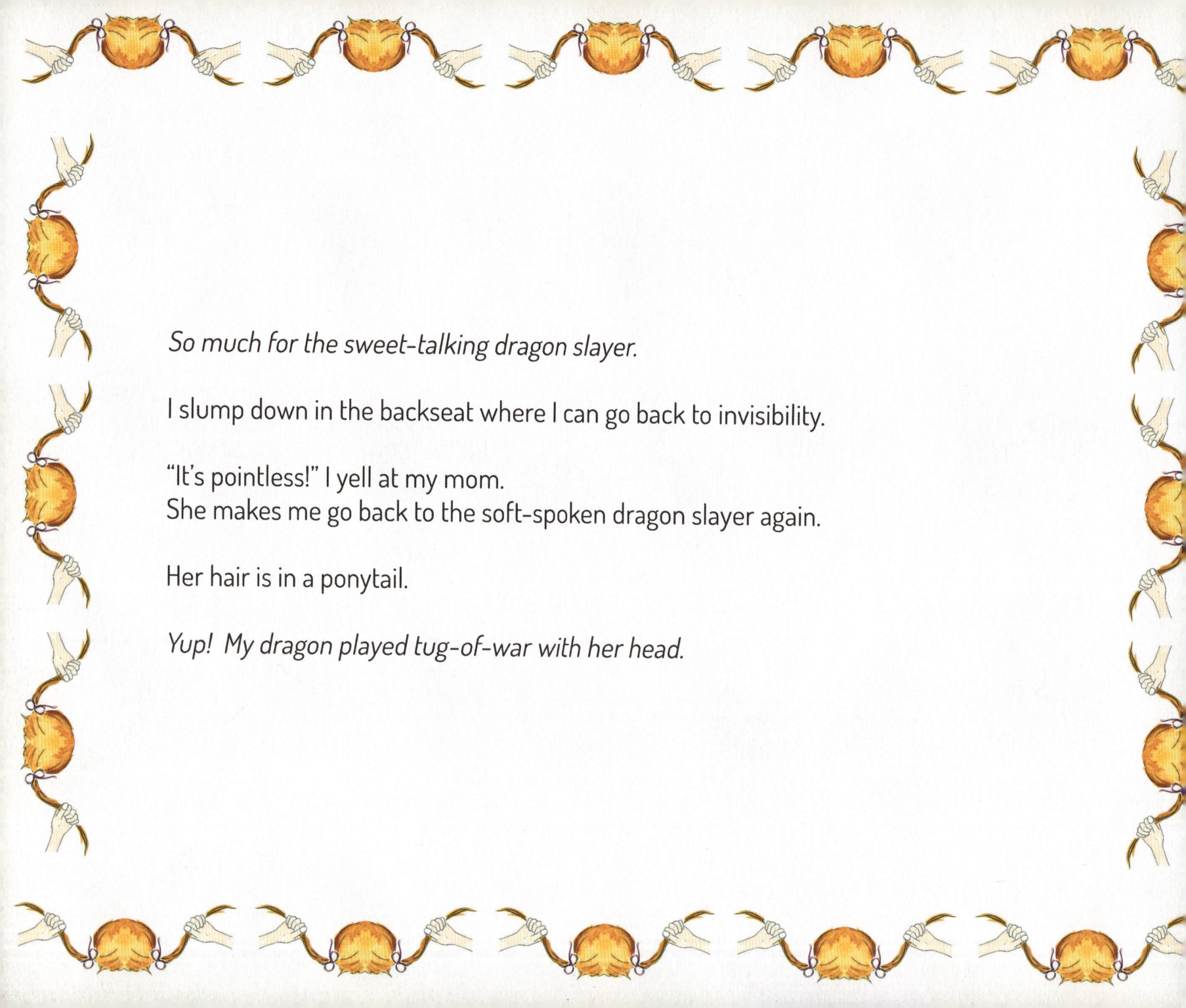

I slump down in the backseat where I can go back to invisibility.

"It's pointless!" I yell at my mom.
She makes me go back to the soft-spoken dragon slayer again.

Her hair is in a ponytail.

Yup! My dragon played tug-of-war with her head.

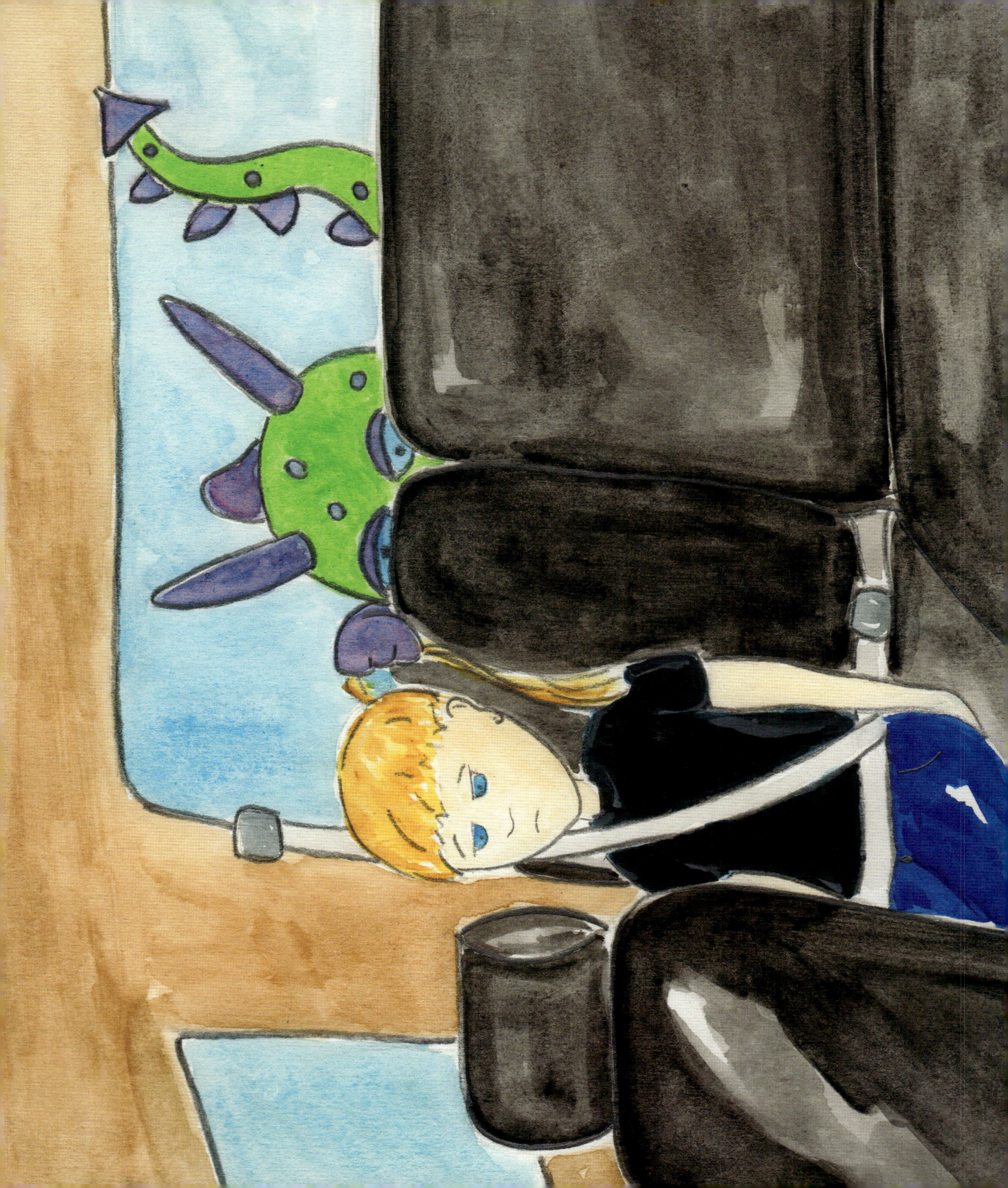

Dumbo, get out … Dumbo, get out … Dumbo, get out …

"So," she says, "how are you?"

"It didn't work. I did what you said. I called him Dumbo and told him to get out, but he wouldn't leave."

"Did you insist?" She leans forward.

"What do you mean?"

"How many times did you tell him to leave?"

"Once, and he said no."

"I'm sorry, I wasn't very clear with you. I didn't mean to make you think that getting rid of him would be easy," she says. "You have to insist, over and over again. Yell at him if you like, but don't argue with him. Tell him to leave and then ignore him."

No! ... No! ... No! ... No! ... No! ... No!

"Dumbo, get out."

No!

I go home and dig in my heels for a long fight. At first I tell him nicely to leave, but he refuses.

The next time I give him my firm voice—the one my mom uses when she gets serious.

He laughs.

I pull out all the stops and yell at him like Mr. Braden, our gym teacher, when the boys get out of control.

"Shut up and get out of my head!"

Dumbo looks shocked.

He starts to argue with me, so I plug my ears and begin to hum a tune in my head.

Every once in awhile I stop and yell at him again.

That night I fall asleep humming that tune, without the dragon in my head.

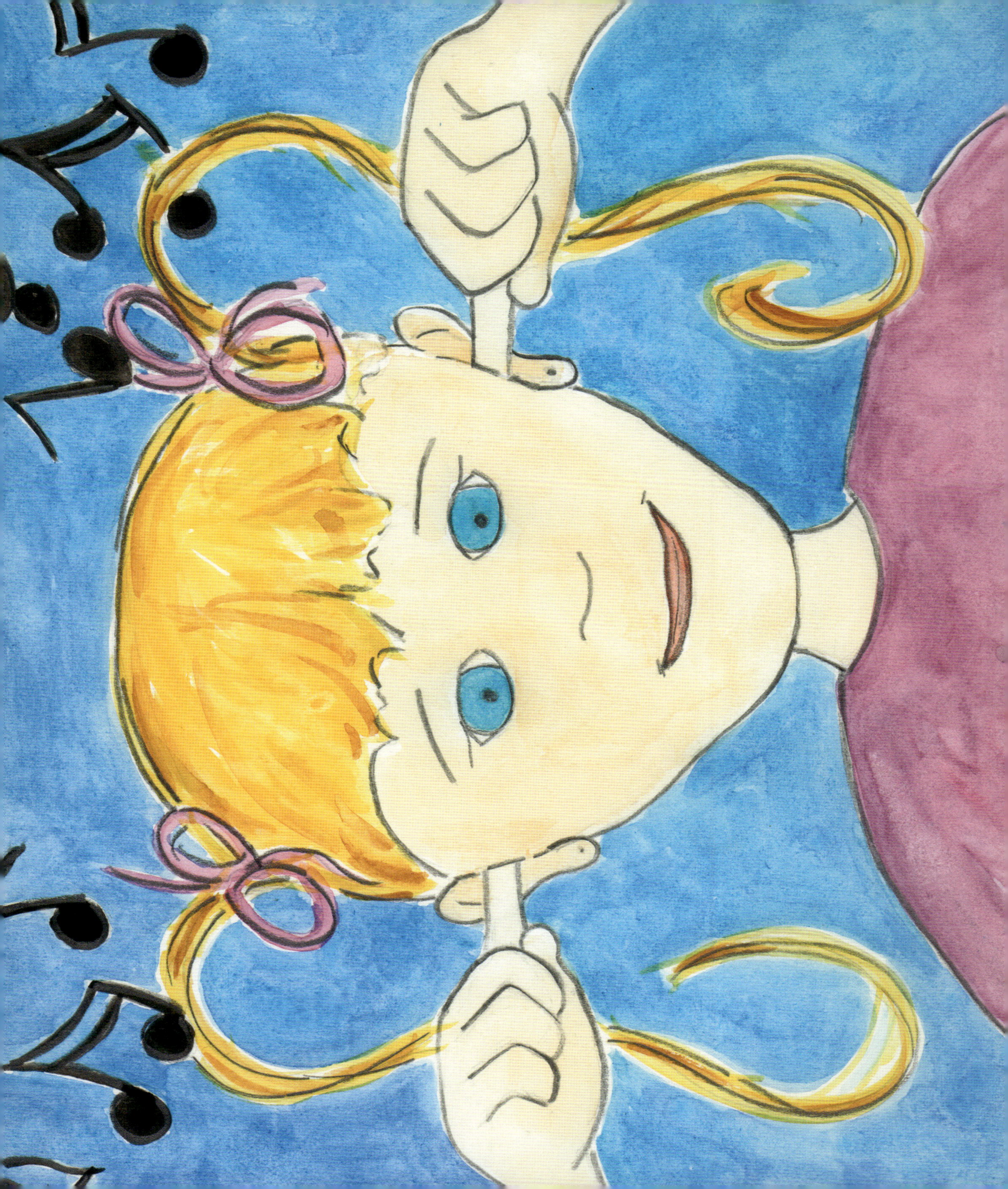

At my next visit with my soft-spoken dragon slayer I report that it is working some of the time, but that Dumbo insists on coming back.

"You didn't think he would give up that easily, did you?"

"Well, I was kind of hoping."

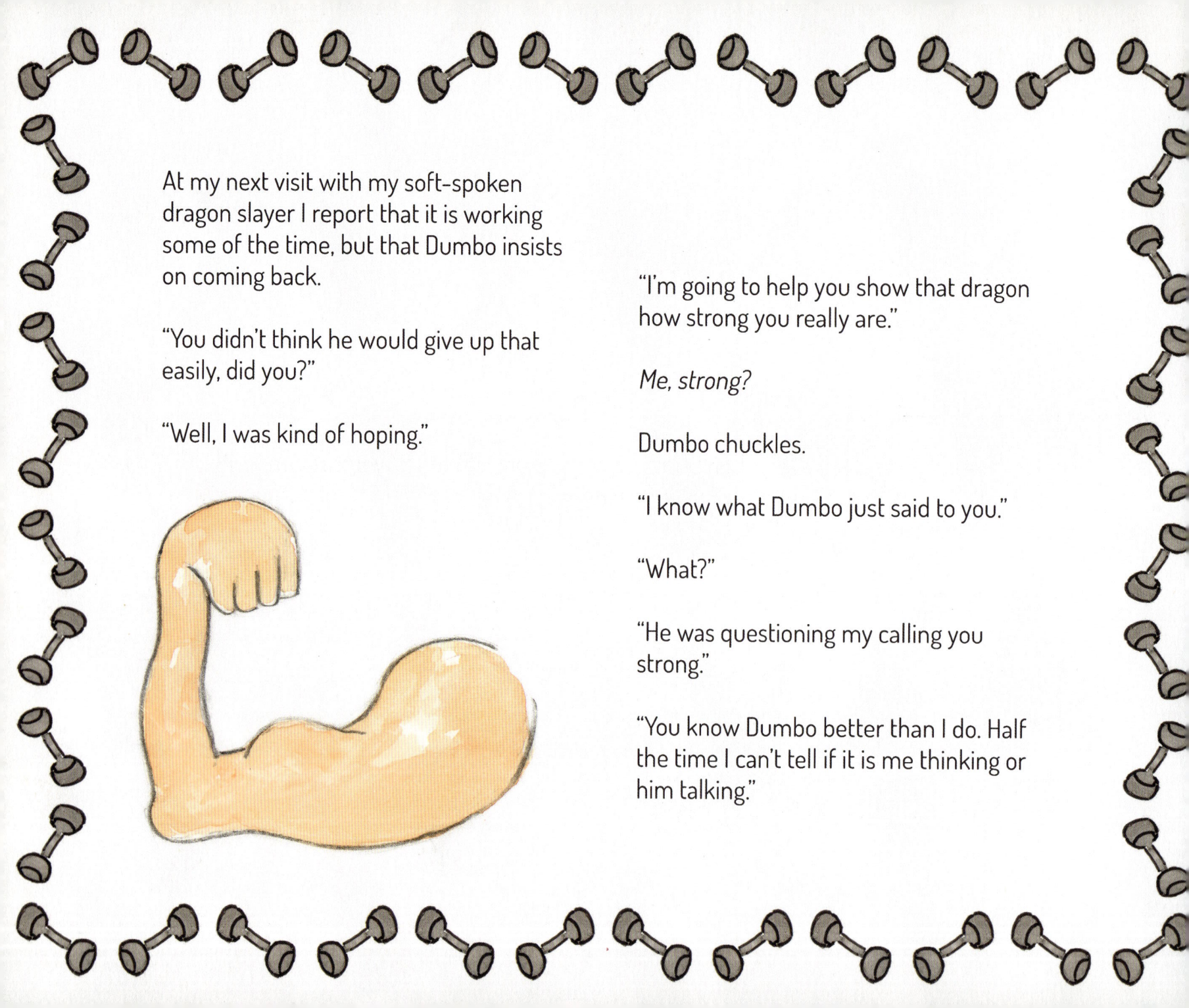

"I'm going to help you show that dragon how strong you really are."

Me, strong?

Dumbo chuckles.

"I know what Dumbo just said to you."

"What?"

"He was questioning my calling you strong."

"You know Dumbo better than I do. Half the time I can't tell if it is me thinking or him talking."

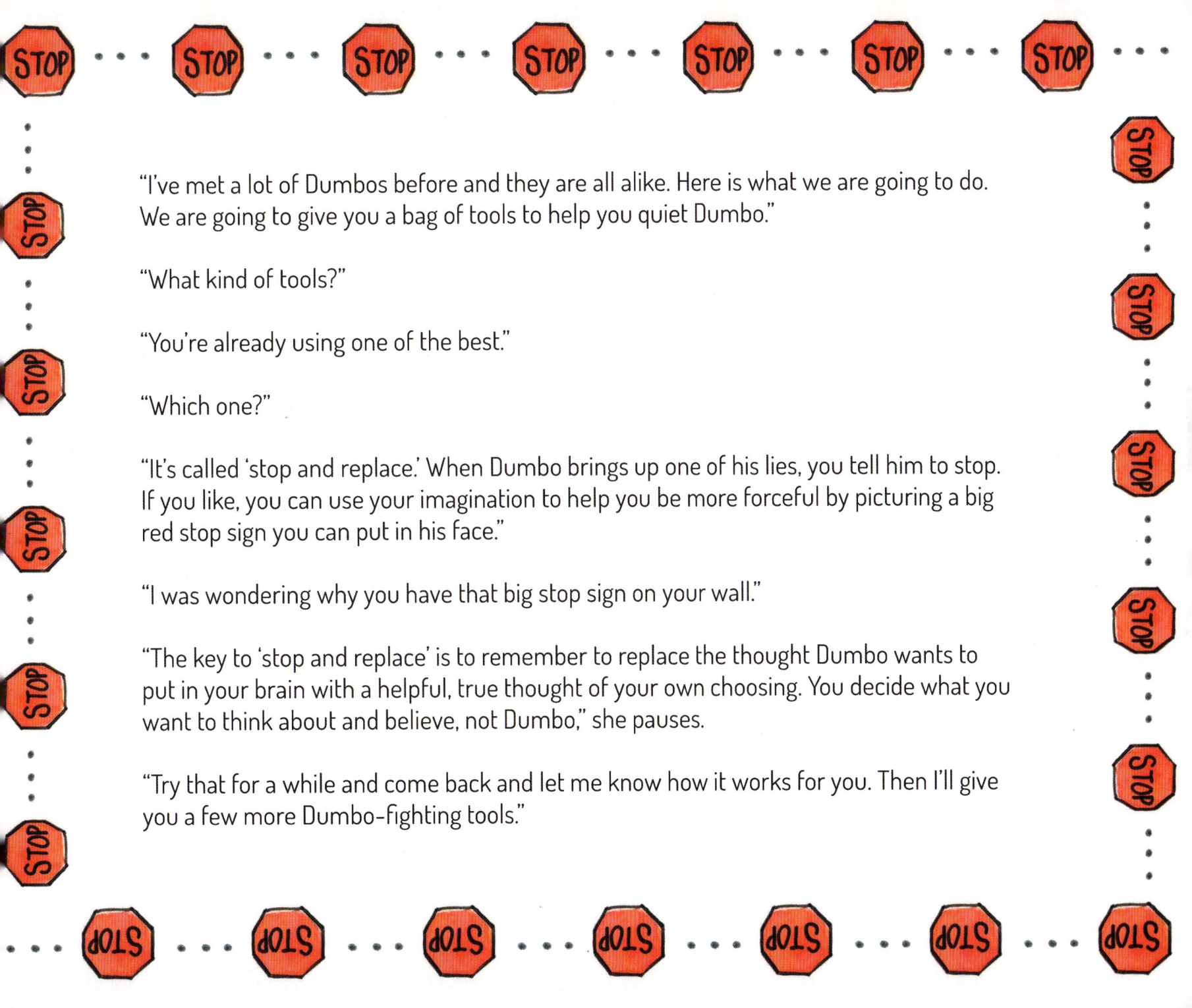

"I've met a lot of Dumbos before and they are all alike. Here is what we are going to do. We are going to give you a bag of tools to help you quiet Dumbo."

"What kind of tools?"

"You're already using one of the best."

"Which one?"

"It's called 'stop and replace.' When Dumbo brings up one of his lies, you tell him to stop. If you like, you can use your imagination to help you be more forceful by picturing a big red stop sign you can put in his face."

"I was wondering why you have that big stop sign on your wall."

"The key to 'stop and replace' is to remember to replace the thought Dumbo wants to put in your brain with a helpful, true thought of your own choosing. You decide what you want to think about and believe, not Dumbo," she pauses.

"Try that for a while and come back and let me know how it works for you. Then I'll give you a few more Dumbo-fighting tools."

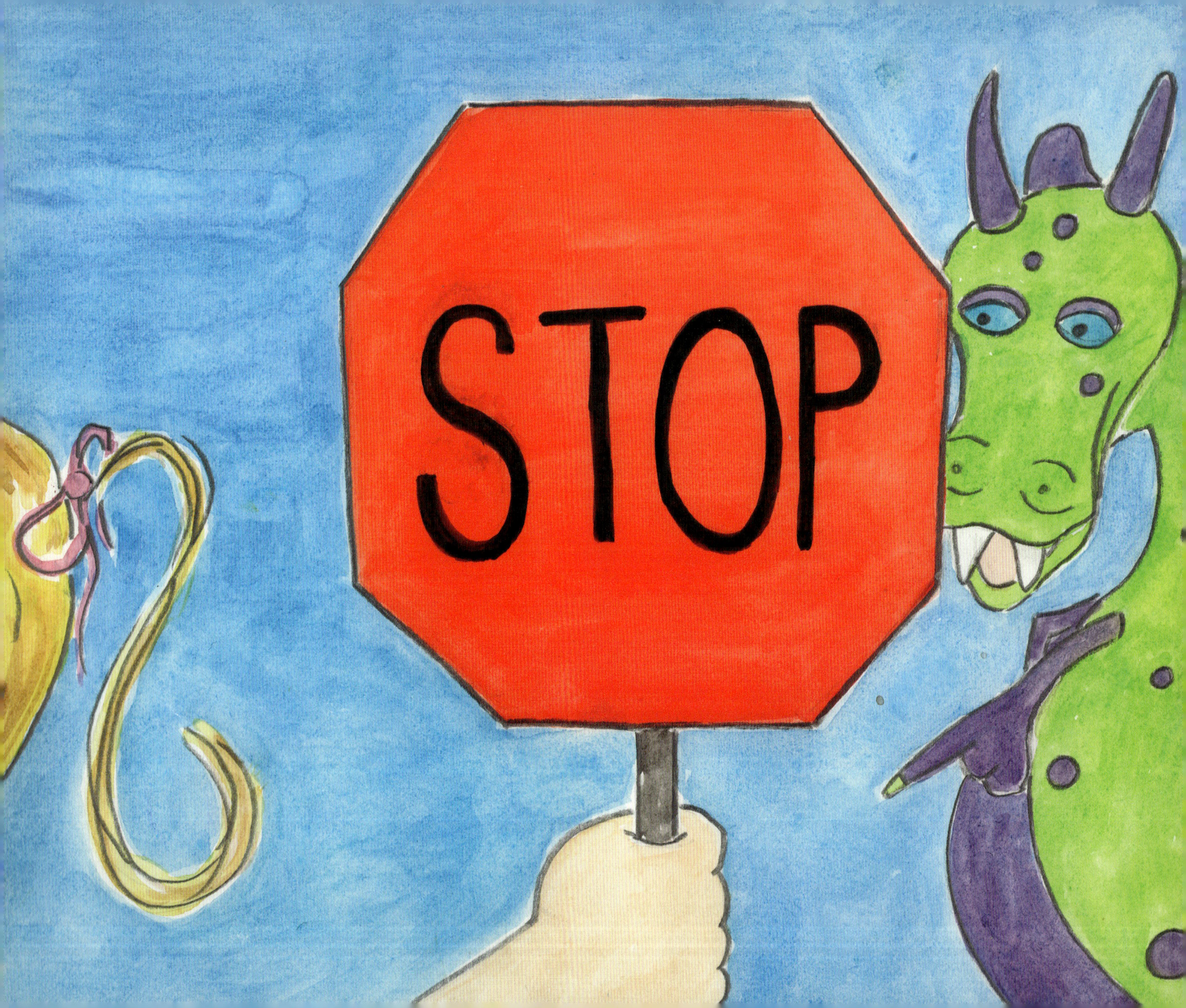
STOP

I have my doubts, but it works.

Every time I put the stop sign in Dumbo's face, his forehead wrinkles and the space between his eyebrows disappears.

He tries to swat it away, but I fill my brain with my own thoughts.

"You're too stupid to think for yourself," he says.

"I get straight A's in school and my teacher says I'm brilliant. That means I'm a shining star," I say.

I picture myself reaching above my head to slap my soft spoken dragon slayer's hand.

"I hate her," he says.

"I know," I say. "That's why I love her."

"It's working," I say to my soft-spoken dragon slayer the next time I see her. "The stop sign is shutting him up."

She smiles and puts up her open palm for a high-five. I smack my palm against hers so hard that it makes both of us wince in pain.

I start to blush, but she laughs, so I join her.

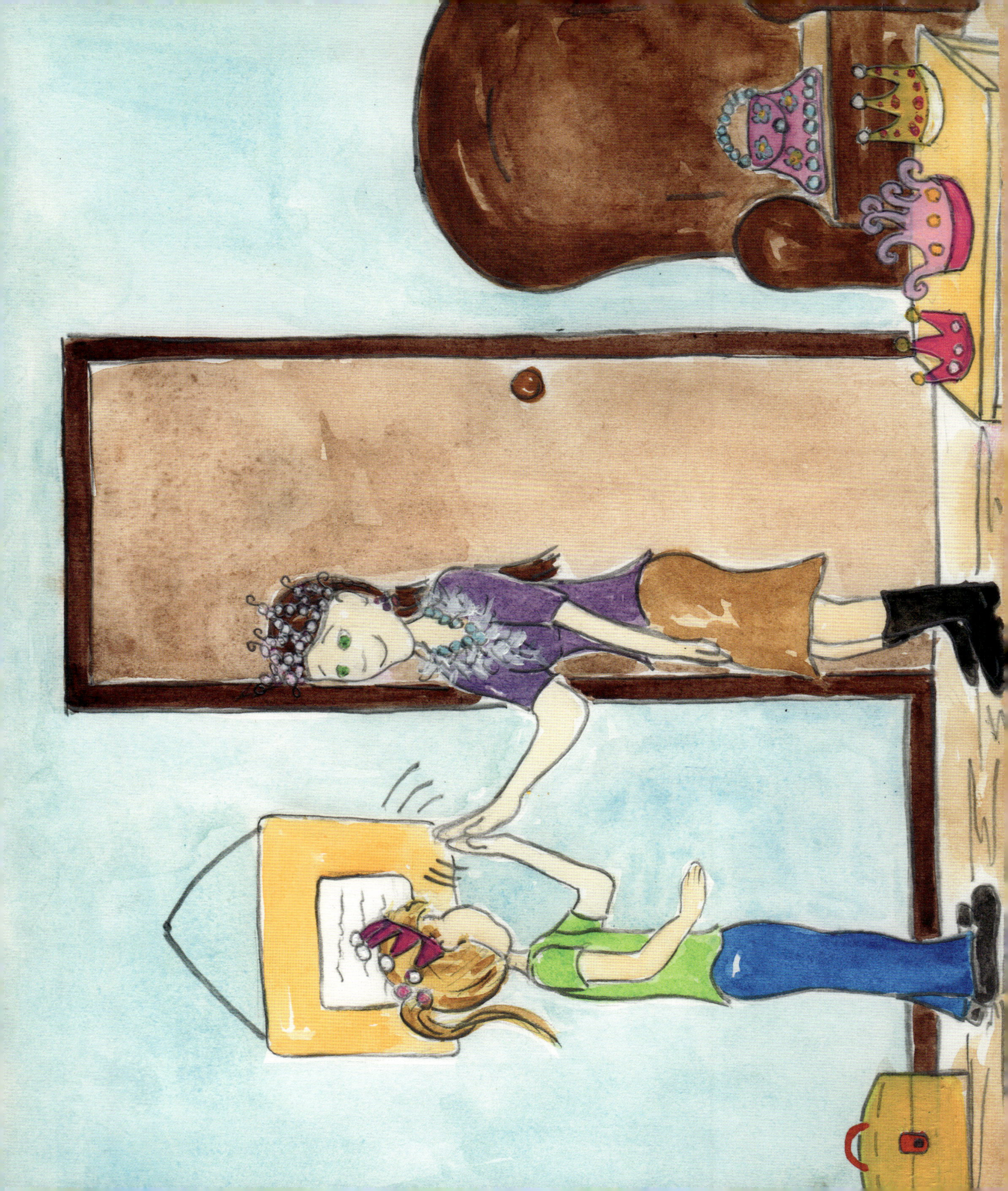

Plan A and Plan B... Plan A and Plan B... Plan A and Plan B... Plan A and Plan B... Plan A and Plan B...

She gives me another tool.

She tells me I always need a Plan A and a Plan B so I won't have to worry about things going wrong.

For example, if I want to play with some girls on the playground and Dumbo tells me not to because they might not want to be my friends, I have to come up with a Plan A and a Plan B.

Plan A will be they say yes and I have a great time.

Plan B will be they say no, so I ask Izzy and Kaley to play. They always say yes so we have a fine time.

My soft-spoken dragon slayer says that when you have two plans, you don't worry so much about one going wrong because you have a back-up.

Guess what—it is true.

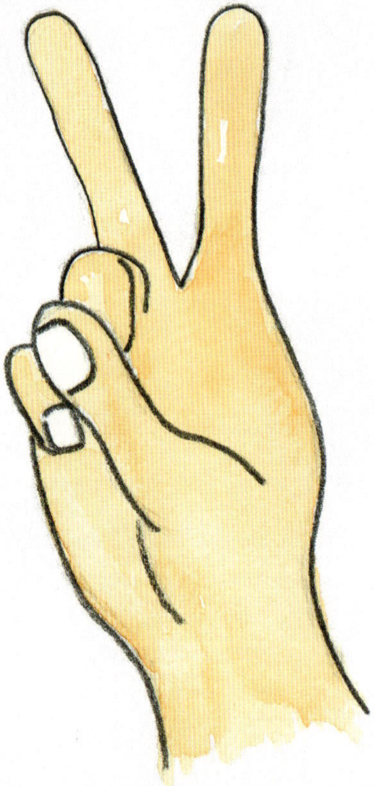

And then what ? ... And then what ? ... And then what ? ...

The next week she adds the And Then What? game to my dragon-slaying toolbox.

That is where you ask someone you trust to help you when you are worried about something.

It goes like this: you tell them what you are worried about and they respond by asking you, "And then what?"

You answer them and they ask you, "And then what?"

You keep repeating this until you have figured out what the worst possible outcome of your worry could be.

What you discover is that it is never as bad as your dragon says it will be.

I mean, it is not like you can die of embarrassment, like your dragon claims.

That's right, I said your dragon.

I know some of you hearing my story have dragons of your own.

After all, I'm not a freak; I'm just a girl with a bad case of the worries.

Are you dying to know what other tools my soft-spoken dragon slayer gave me?

Well, here is my favorite.

She calls it deep breathing. I call it blowing your dragon away.

Breathing deeply tells your body to relax.

That is a good thing when you are worried, because it is the opposite of what your dragon wants you to be doing.

He wants you to freak out.

The best way to stop your dragon is to stop and take ten slow, deep breaths through your nose.

You should try it, it really calms you down.

I've added my own twist to this tool.

While I'm breathing deeply, I pretend to look my dragon in the eyes and when I breathe out, I blow him away from me until he is so far away I can't see him anymore.

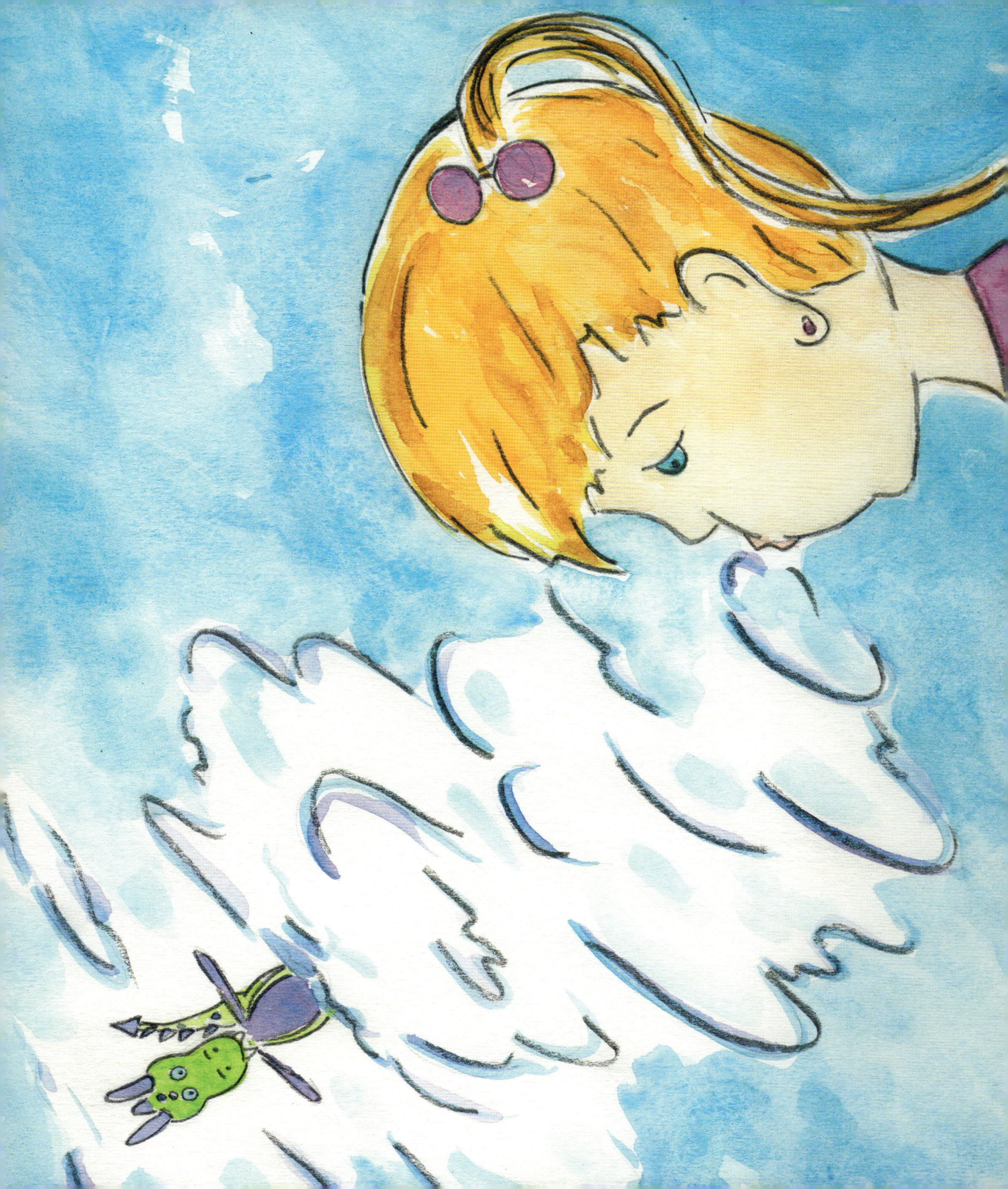

Do you want to know all the tools in my soft-spoken dragon slayer's toolbox?

There are a lot of them and I don't have time to tell you about them all right now.

I have to get to the end of my story so I can get back to my new dragon-free life.

But I'll email you a list after I'm done, so you can pick your favorites!

You don't want your toolbox to get too heavy or you won't be able to carry it around with you.

Especially if you are like me and you want to carry your tools in a sequin purse covered with flowery designs.

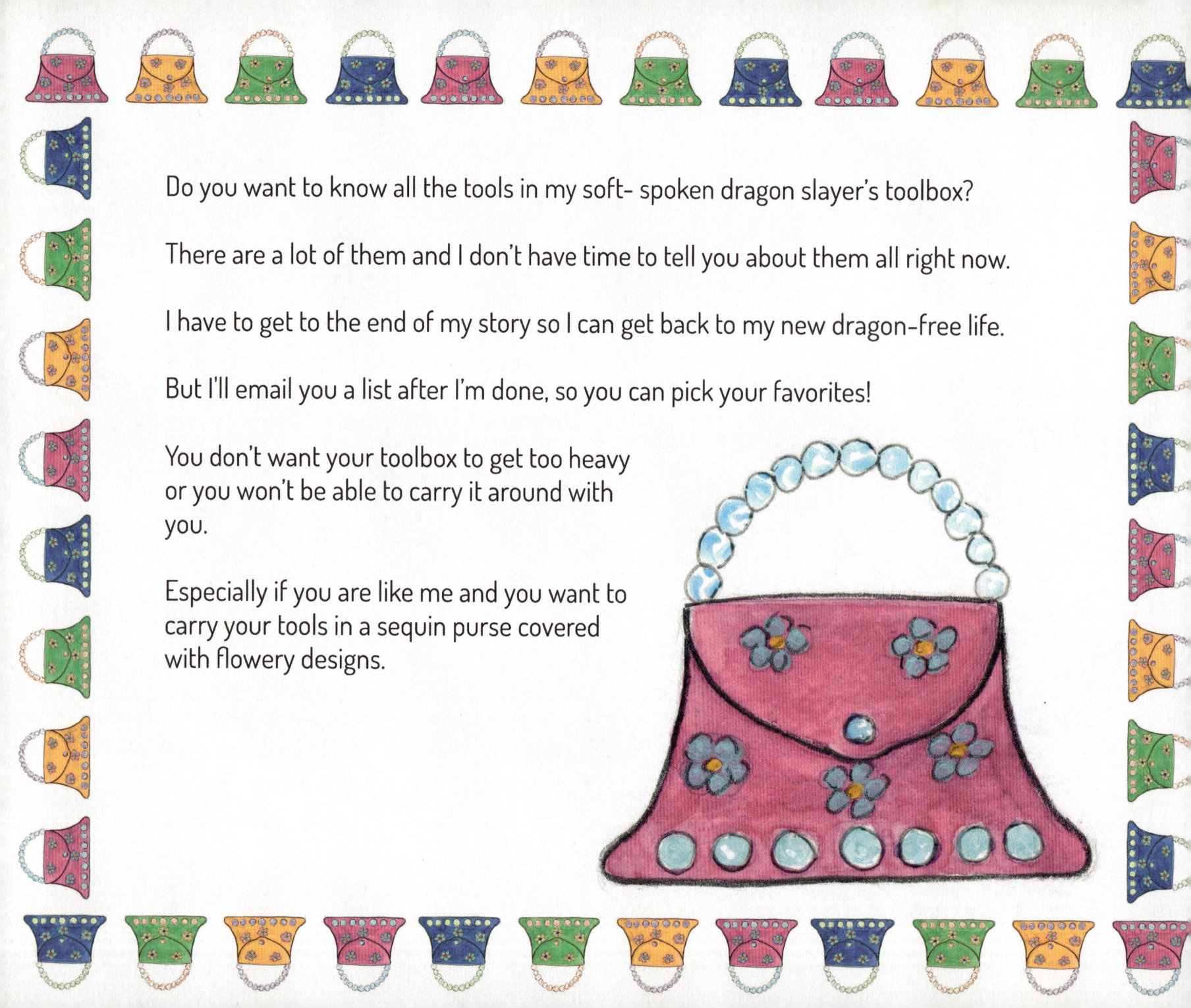

I finally go for my last visit to my soft-spoken dragon slayer.

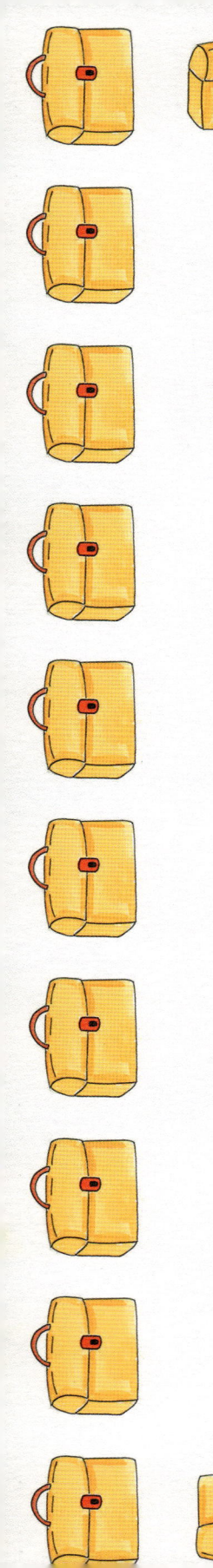

I am dressed in a beautiful fluffy skirt with a lot of ruffles and a shiny top with tons of sparkles.

My hair is in pigtails tied with gemstone hair pieces.

I am a bit afraid of saying goodbye to my dragon slayer.

"What if Dumbo comes back?" I ask.

"Mark my words, he will try."

"Can't you make him go away forever?"

"I'm afraid that is beyond our power, but I can assure you that when he does try to come back, you will be ready with your bag of tools and you will send him away again."

She assures me Plan B is in place – I can come back anytime I need help with Dumbo.

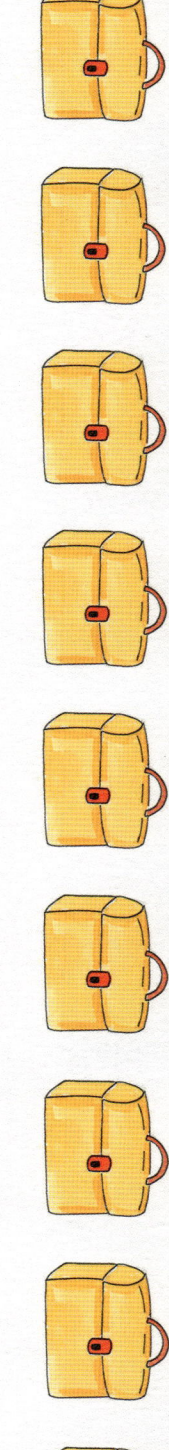

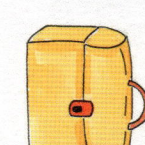

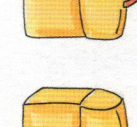

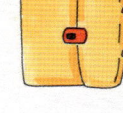

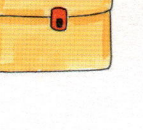

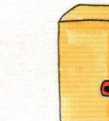

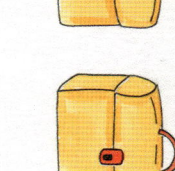

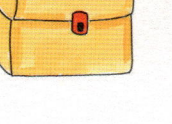

We make tea and eat fancy cookies.

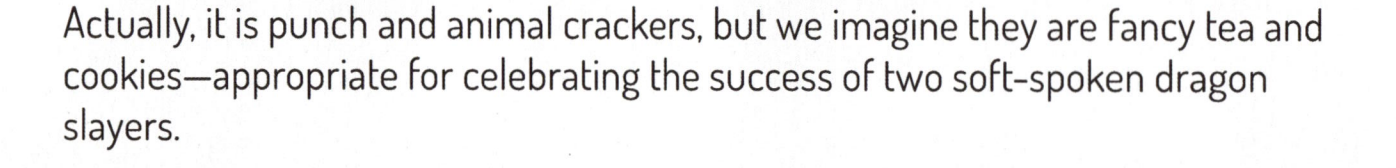

Actually, it is punch and animal crackers, but we imagine they are fancy tea and cookies—appropriate for celebrating the success of two soft-spoken dragon slayers.

While we are talking and laughing, my soft-spoken dragon slayer stands up.

"This celebration needs a victory dance. Come join me in the dance of joy around the coffee table. It's a tradition I've started every time a new dragon slayer is born."

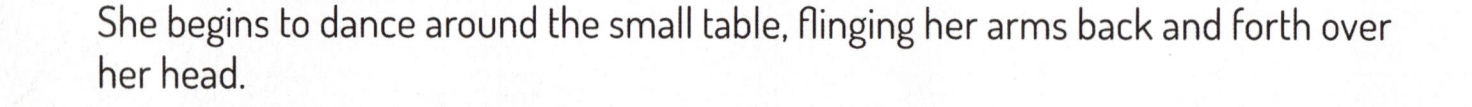

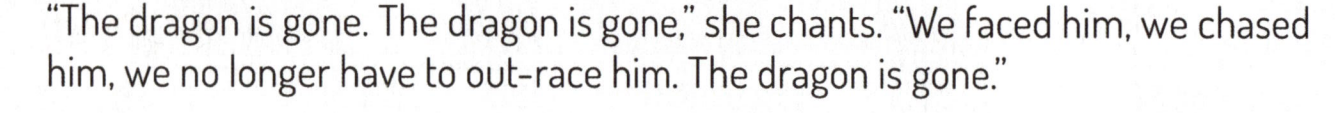

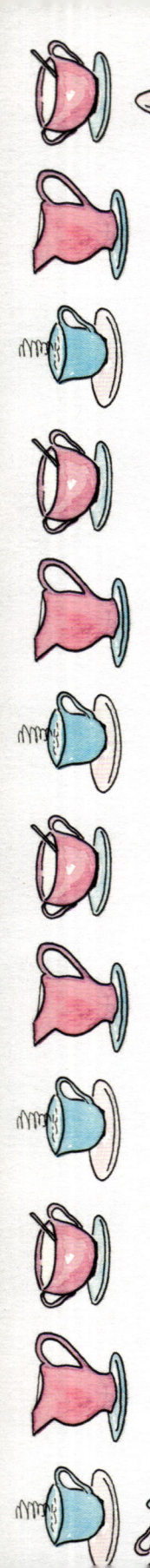

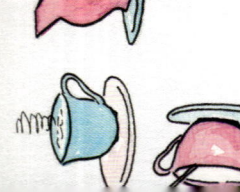

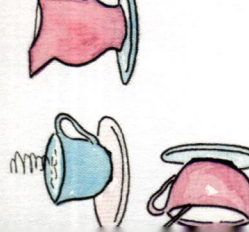

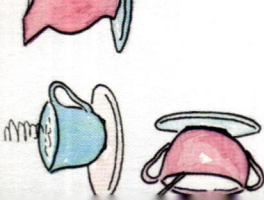

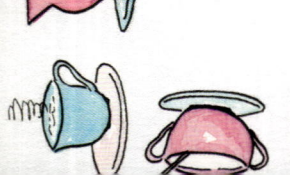

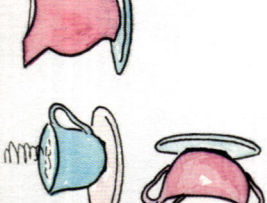

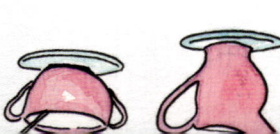

She begins to dance around the small table, flinging her arms back and forth over her head.

"The dragon is gone. The dragon is gone," she chants. "We faced him, we chased him, we no longer have to out-race him. The dragon is gone."

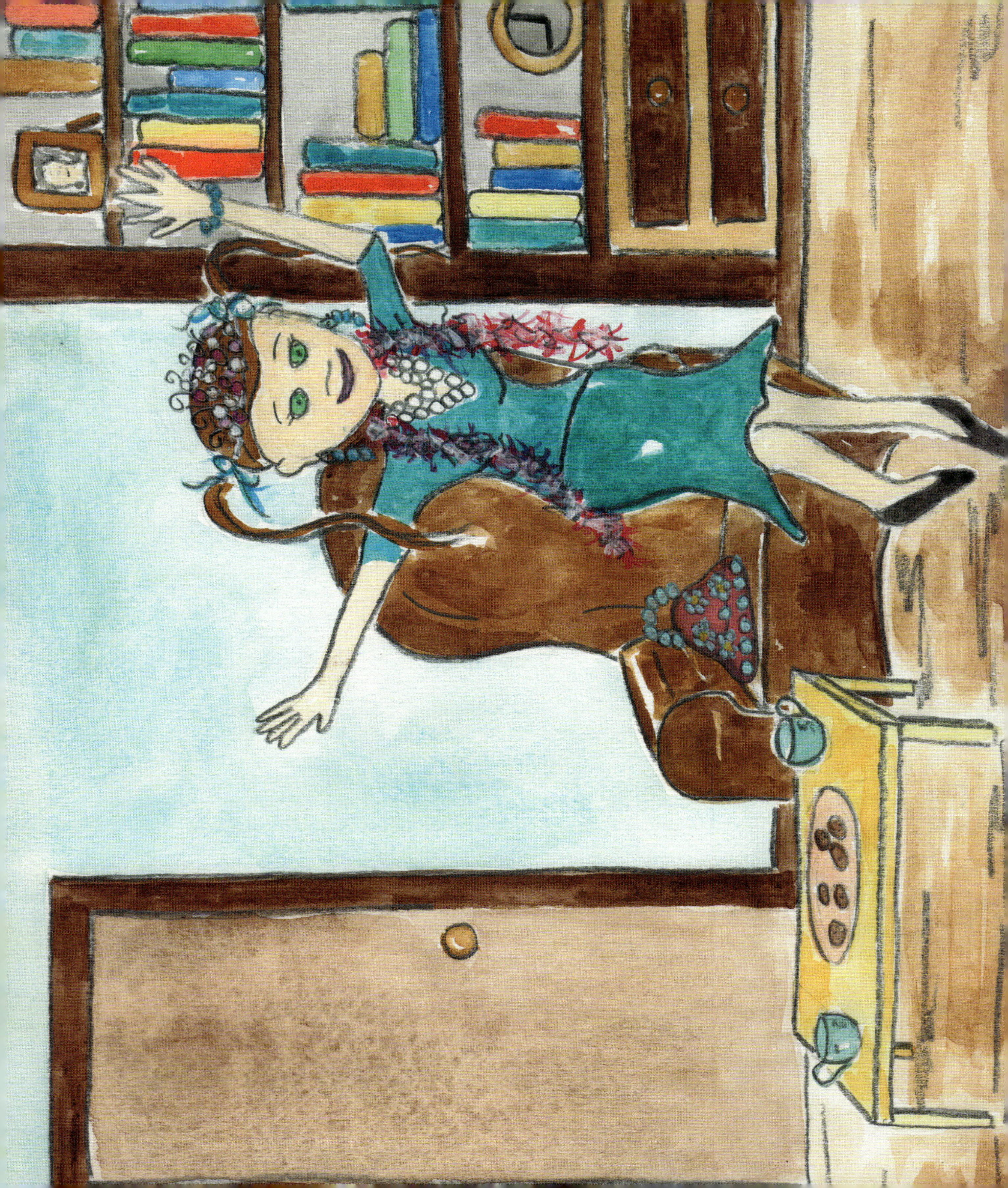

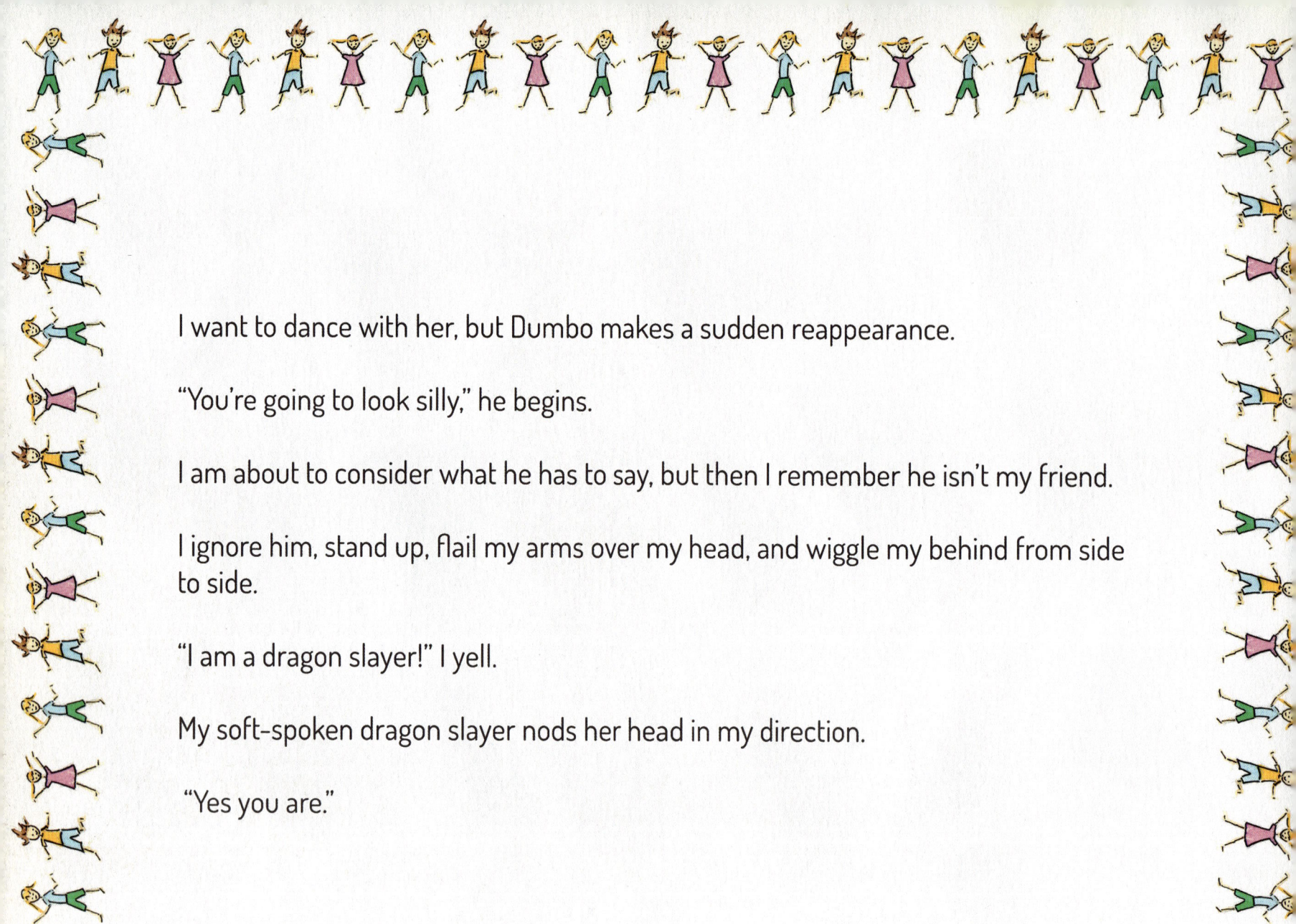

I want to dance with her, but Dumbo makes a sudden reappearance.

"You're going to look silly," he begins.

I am about to consider what he has to say, but then I remember he isn't my friend.

I ignore him, stand up, flail my arms over my head, and wiggle my behind from side to side.

"I am a dragon slayer!" I yell.

My soft-spoken dragon slayer nods her head in my direction.

"Yes you are."

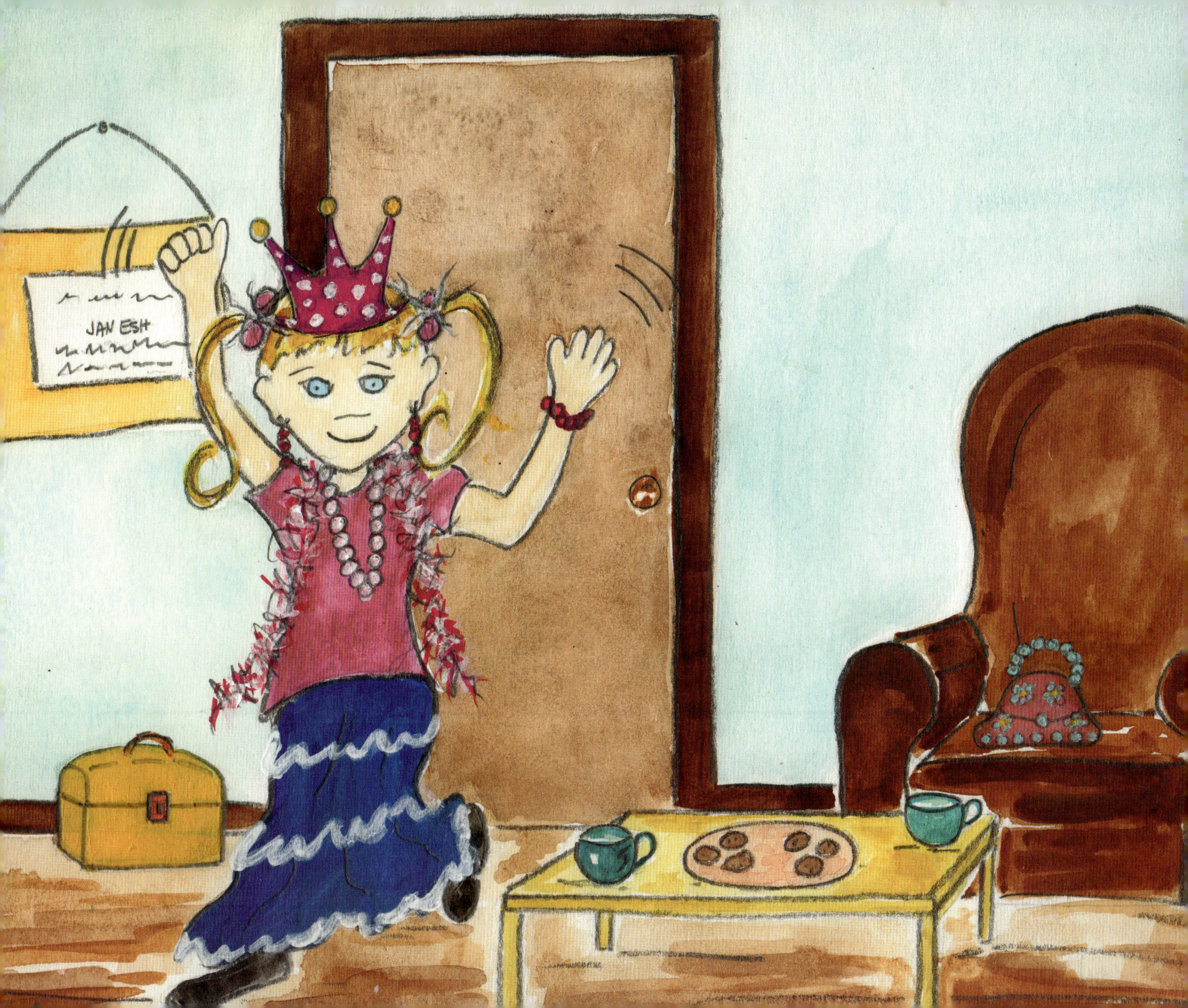
JAN ESH

NEW MESSAGE
To: myfellowdragonslayers@worryfree.com
From: newestdragonslayer@worryfree.com
CC:
Subject: toolbox / fancy purse

All dragon slayers need a toolbox or fancy purse filled with ideas on how to overcome the dragon in their head. That way, when a crisis arises and the dragon is on the attack, they can look inside and pick one or two strategies to help keep him in his place. Here are some examples.

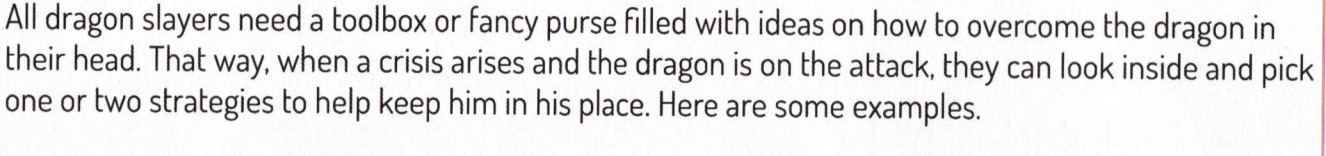

• Find yourself a soft spoken dragon slayer of your own who has experience helping people learn how to slay the dragon in their head.

• Get the dragon out of your head so you hear him better and can tell his voice from yours. Give him a name. Yell at him.

• Let him know you choose your friends and he isn't one of them. Tell him to "shut up." Don't worry if it sounds mean. He is a dragon and deserves it.

• Your parents won't be disappointed in you. They want you to stop listening to your dragon.

• Take deep breaths through your nose and blow your dragon right out of the room.

• Stop your dragon's worry thoughts (lies) and replace them with your own truthful thoughts.

• Always have Plan A and Plan B.

• Play the "And Then What?" game.

• Exercise when you get worried. Go for a walk, run up and down the stairs, dance like a wild person, or spin yourself in a circle until you get dizzy.

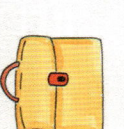

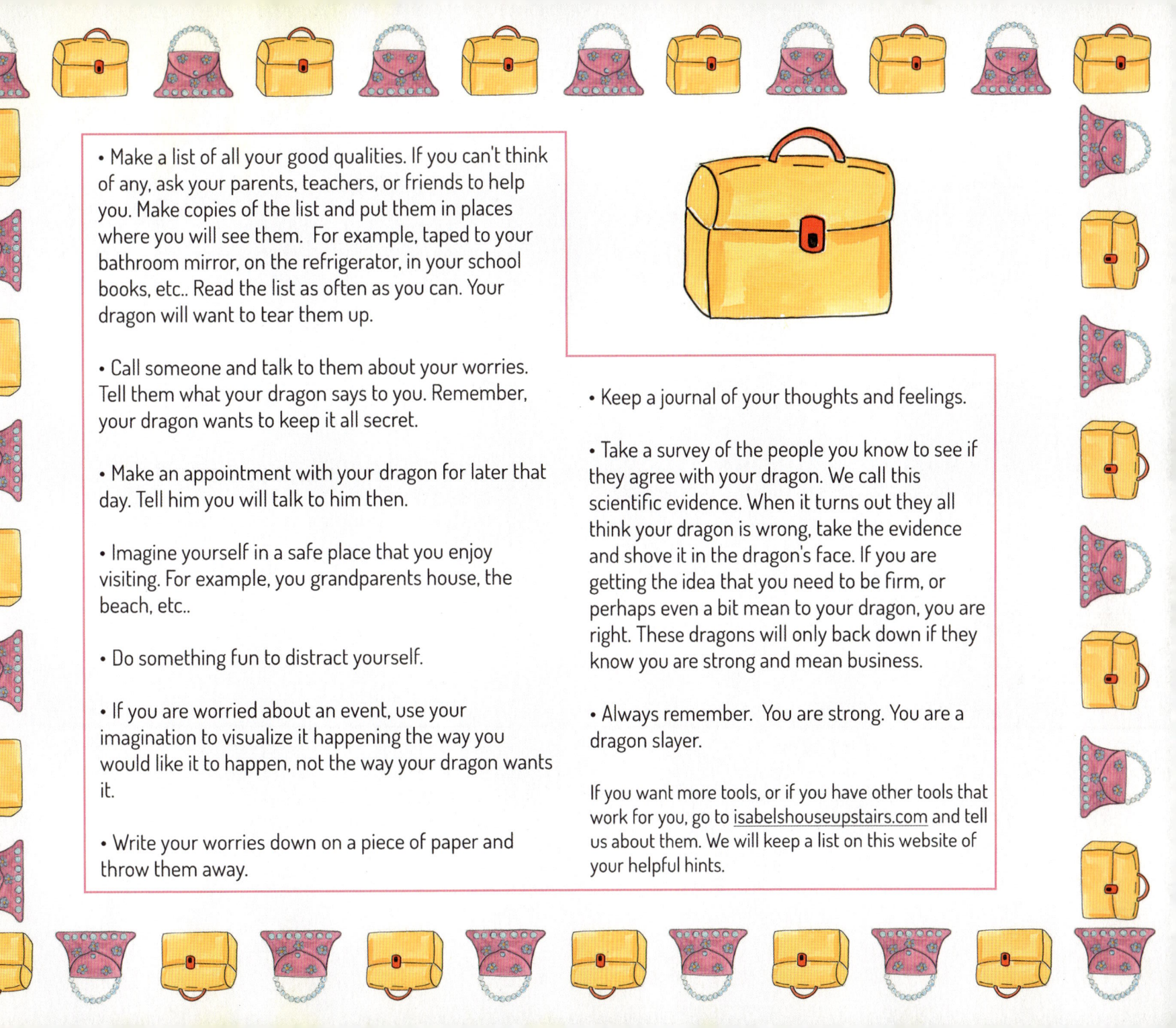

- Keep a journal of your thoughts and feelings.

- Take a survey of the people you know to see if they agree with your dragon. We call this scientific evidence. When it turns out they all think your dragon is wrong, take the evidence and shove it in the dragon's face. If you are getting the idea that you need to be firm, or perhaps even a bit mean to your dragon, you are right. These dragons will only back down if they know you are strong and mean business.

- Always remember. You are strong. You are a dragon slayer.

If you want more tools, or if you have other tools that work for you, go to isabelshouseupstairs.com and tell us about them. We will keep a list on this website of your helpful hints.

- Make a list of all your good qualities. If you can't think of any, ask your parents, teachers, or friends to help you. Make copies of the list and put them in places where you will see them. For example, taped to your bathroom mirror, on the refrigerator, in your school books, etc.. Read the list as often as you can. Your dragon will want to tear them up.

- Call someone and talk to them about your worries. Tell them what your dragon says to you. Remember, your dragon wants to keep it all secret.

- Make an appointment with your dragon for later that day. Tell him you will talk to him then.

- Imagine yourself in a safe place that you enjoy visiting. For example, you grandparents house, the beach, etc..

- Do something fun to distract yourself.

- If you are worried about an event, use your imagination to visualize it happening the way you would like it to happen, not the way your dragon wants it.

- Write your worries down on a piece of paper and throw them away.

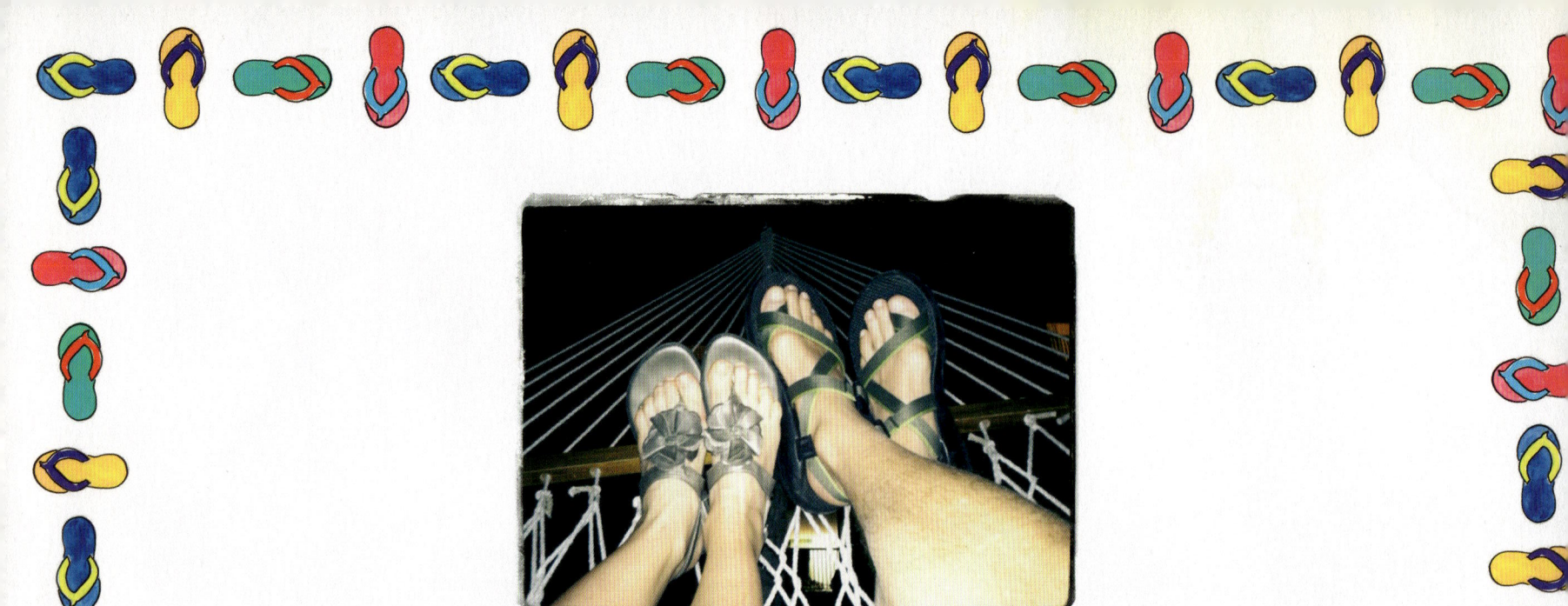

Janice Esh and Stephen Nauta are psychotherapists at Isabel's House in Spring Lake, Michigan. Combined they have over fifty years of experience treating children and adults with anxiety disorders. They have a love of children's literature because of the power these books have to influence young minds. Anxiety tends to be a family affair, meaning that parents who bring their children in for treatment often discover their own struggles with the disorder. Steve and Jan can think of no better way for families to deal with anxiety than to share a children's book that offers hope through a proven method of therapy for the treatment of anxiety in all ages. For more information on Jan and Steve visit isabelshousecounseling.com or for more on this book visit isabelshouseupstairs.com.

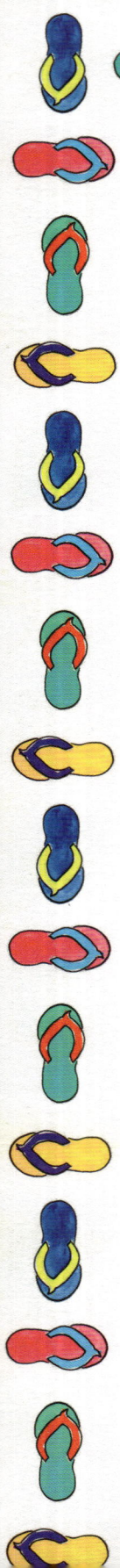

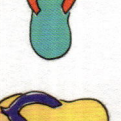

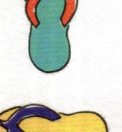

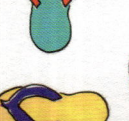

Professional Artist Christi Dreese was born and raised in West Michigan and has been involved in the arts since she was a child. She spent summers as a young girl on her father's boat coasting along Lake Michigan. It was there she grew to love the calm waters, sunsets, and relaxed atmosphere. Many of her oil paintings are inspired by the Lake Michigan coastline.

Along with Christi's passion for the lakeshore, she has found abstract to be a great emotional release and different creative process from her impressionistic landscapes. Every work of art is inspired by her thoughts and feelings.

Christi received her Bachelor of Art degree at Aquinas College in Grand Rapids, emphasizing in painting, and also attained a business administration major.

Christi's love for the arts, lakeshore and personal growth continues to inspire her to create new works of art and have purpose in life.

www.dreesefineart.com